GCSE Music
The Revision Guide

- **Also perfect for grade exams**

- **Clear and concise**

- **99.8% X Factor free**

Published by CGP

Main Author:
Elena Delaney

Further Contributors:
Catherine Baird, Polly Cotterill, Chris Dennett, Rob Hall, Peter Maries, Katherine Reed,
Glenn Rogers, Julie Wakeling, Caley Simpson, Claire Thompson.

With thanks to Nikki Ball and Katherine Craig for the proofreading.

ISBN: 978 1 84762 366 9

www.cgpbooks.co.uk
Clipart from Corel®
Printed by Elanders Ltd, Newcastle upon Tyne

Based on the classic CGP style created by Richard Parsons.

Text, design, layout and original illustrations © Coordination Group Publications Ltd. (CGP) 2009
All rights reserved.

Photocopying more than one chapter of this book is not permitted. Extra copies are available from CGP.
0870 750 1242 • www.cgpbooks.co.uk

Contents

SECTION 1 — THE BASICS

You might <u>know</u> the stuff on this page already. Then again you might <u>think</u> you know it all but be wrong about a couple of things. Or you might think you don't know <u>anything</u> when in fact you know <u>everything</u>. There's <u>only one way</u> to find out. Read it all and <u>learn it</u> before you carry on.

① CLEF

These swirly symbols at the start tell you how <u>high</u> or <u>low</u> to play the notes. All the different clefs are covered on <u>page 4</u>.

② NOTE

Each note is shown by a separate <u>oval</u>. The symbol also tells you how <u>long</u> or <u>short</u> the note is. The symbols are shown on <u>page 8</u>.

③ TWO LINES OF MUSIC

The top line of music has got a tune — it's the <u>MELOD</u>. The bottom line is the <u>ACCOMPANIMENT</u>.

⑨ TIME SIGNATURE

The numbers tell you about the <u>beats</u> in a bar. Time signatures are covered on <u>page 6</u>.

⑪ BEATS

Each bar has the <u>same</u> number of <u>BEATS</u>. Beats, bars and rhythm are covered on <u>pages 6 & 7</u>.

⑩ KEY SIGNATURE

There are no flats or sharps, so this piece is in the <u>KEY</u> of C. Keys and scales are covered in <u>Section 3</u>.

⑫ STRUCTURE

The melody's built out of two different tunes — phrases and structures are covered in <u>Section</u>

THE PIANO KEYBOARD

Some of the diagrams in this book make more sense if you know what's what on a <u>piano keyboard</u>. The white keys play <u>NATURAL NOTES</u>.

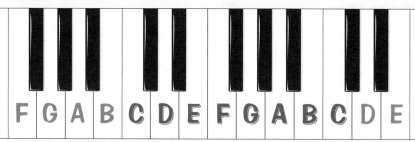

Note: The white notes from C to C make the scale of C major (p.15).

The black keys play <u>SHARPS</u> and <u>FLATS</u>. Sharps and flats are covered on <u>page 5</u>.

The C right in the centre of a piano keyboard is known as <u>MIDDLE C</u>.

5 **LEMON**
A shiny yellow <u>fruit</u>.

6 **SAILOR**
Ahoy there.

7 **STAVE**
The five lines are called a <u>stave</u>. Notes can go <u>on</u> or <u>between</u> the lines, or on separate short lines above or below.

BAR
The vertical bar lines split the music into <u>bars</u>.

bar line

8 **TRIPLETS**
The three along with the curved line shows these notes are <u>triplets</u>. They're explained on <u>page 9</u>.

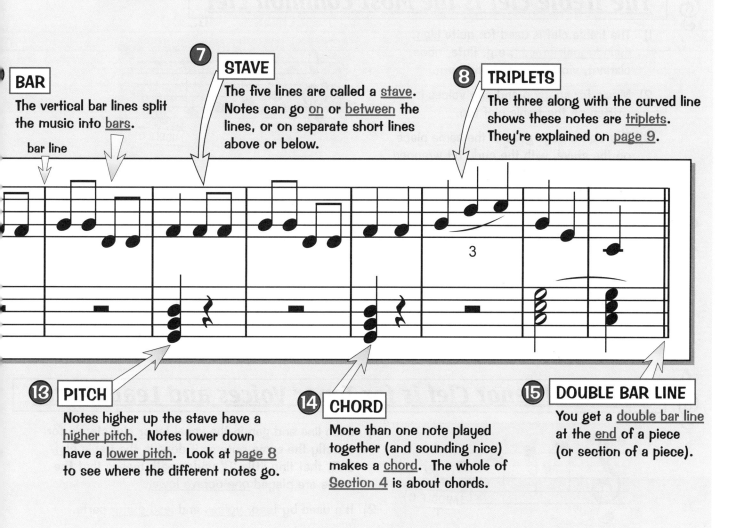

3

13 **PITCH**
Notes higher up the stave have a <u>higher pitch</u>. Notes lower down have a <u>lower pitch</u>. Look at <u>page 8</u> to see where the different notes go.

14 **CHORD**
More than one note played together (and sounding nice) makes a <u>chord</u>. The whole of <u>Section 4</u> is about chords.

15 **DOUBLE BAR LINE**
You get a <u>double bar line</u> at the <u>end</u> of a piece (or section of a piece).

TONES AND SEMITONES

<u>TONES</u> and <u>SEMITONES</u> are the gaps between notes.

On a piano, a <u>SEMITONE</u> is the gap between any key, <u>black or white</u>, and its immediate neighbour.

The gap from any key to a key <u>two semitone steps</u> above or below is called a <u>TONE</u>.

semitone   semitone

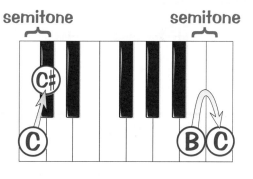

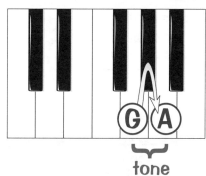

tone

Clefs

Clefs are the squiggly symbols that you find right at the start of most written music.
The treble clef's used for high-pitched music. The bass and alto clefs are used for lower-pitched music.

The Treble Clef is the Most Common Clef

1) The treble clef is used for quite high, melody instruments, e.g. flute, oboe, clarinet, violin, trumpet and horn.

2) Music for soprano and alto voices is written on the treble clef too.

3) The sign always goes in the same place on the stave, with the curly bit wrapped around the line for the G above middle C.

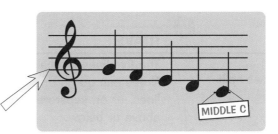

The Bass Clef is used for Low, Bass Instruments

1) The bass clef is used for low instruments like the tuba, trombone, bassoon, cello and double bass.

2) It's also used for bass voices.

3) The big blob always goes on the line for the F below middle C, and the two little dots go either side of the line.

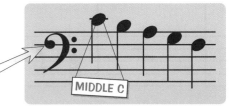

The Vocal Tenor Clef is for Tenor Voices and Lead Guitar

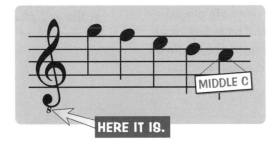

1) Each line and gap in the vocal tenor clef stands for exactly the same note as it does in the treble clef, BUT, that tiny little '8' underneath means that the notes are played one octave lower.

2) It's used by tenor voices and lead guitar parts.

The C Clef can Move Up and Down on the Stave

The C clef always has its middle point on middle C. It can be used as 2 different clefs, depending on its position on the stave.

1) When its middle point is on the middle line, it's the alto clef and is used for viola parts.

2) When the middle point is on the fourth line up, it's called the tenor clef. It's used for the higher notes in bass instruments like trombones, bassoons and cellos.

There'll be blue birds over... the white clefs of Dover...

You'll probably be used to reading just one clef (or two if you're a pianist), but you need to know them all. Make sure you know where middle C is on each clef. Aim to get so good at reading and writing on the treble and bass clefs that you can do it in a plague of thunderflies. They're written out in full on page 8.

Sharps, Flats & Naturals

On a piano, <u>natural</u> notes are the <u>white</u> ones. <u>Sharps</u> are the <u>black</u> notes to the <u>right</u> of the white notes. <u>Flats</u> are the <u>black</u> notes to the <u>left</u> of the white notes. So each black note is both sharp <u>and</u> flat. Clever stuff.

♯ A Sharp Makes a Note Slightly Higher

1) A sharp sign next to a note tells you to play it <u>one semitone higher</u>.

When you're writing on the stave, put sharps, flats and naturals <u>before</u> the note they affect. If you're writing text, put them <u>afterwards</u> — F#.

2) A <u>double sharp</u> — 𝄪 — makes a note <u>two semitones higher</u>. If you see <u>C𝄪</u> you play <u>D</u> — it's the <u>same note</u> going by a different name.

The fancy name for notes that sound the same but have different names is <u>enharmonic equivalents</u>.

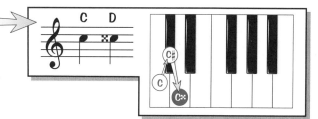

♭ A Flat Makes a Note Lower

1) A flat symbol next to a note means you have to play it <u>one semitone lower</u>.

2) A <u>double flat</u> — (♭♭) — makes a note two semitones (a tone) lower.

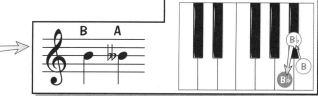

The Key Signature's Shown with Sharps or Flats

KEY SIGNATURE

This key signature's got one sharp — on the <u>F line</u>. You have to play <u>every</u> F in the piece as an <u>F♯</u>.

1) Sharps or flats written at the <u>start</u> of a piece, straight after the clef, tell you the <u>key signature</u>.

2) The key signature makes notes sharp or flat <u>all the way through</u> a piece of music.

3) Sharps and flats that you see by individual notes — but not in the key signature — are called <u>accidentals</u>. Once an accidental has appeared in a bar, it applies to all notes of the same pitch for the <u>rest of the bar</u>, unless it's cancelled out by a <u>natural sign</u>...

> More about key signatures on p.15.

A Natural Sign Cancels a Sharp or Flat

A <u>natural</u> sign before a note <u>cancels</u> the <u>effect of a sharp or flat</u> sign from earlier in the bar or from a key signature.

You <u>never</u> see natural signs in the music, as <u>accidentals</u>.

This stuff should all come naturally in no time...

Double sharps and flats are very <u>rare</u> and quite weird — it doesn't seem that <u>logical</u> to write C𝄪 when you could write D. It all depends what key you're in. Strange, but then that's music for you.

Time Signatures

Those <u>two numbers</u> at the beginning of a piece of music tell you <u>how many beats</u> there are in a bar and <u>how long</u> they are. If you ignore them, whatever you're playing just sounds like a <u>gloopy mess</u>.

Music Has a <u>Regular Beat</u>

1) You can tap your foot along to the <u>beat</u> of any piece of music, so long as it hasn't got a horribly complicated rhythm. The beat is also called the <u>pulse</u>.

2) If you listen a bit harder, you can hear that some beats are <u>stronger</u> than others.

3) The strong beats come at <u>regular intervals</u> — usually every <u>2</u>, <u>3</u> or <u>4</u> beats.

4) The strong beat is the <u>first</u> beat of each <u>bar</u>. If the strong beat comes every 3 beats, then the piece of music you're listening to has <u>three beats</u> in a bar.

The <u>Time Signature</u> Shows How Many Beats in a Bar

1) There's always a <u>time signature</u> at the beginning of a piece of music.

2) It goes to the <u>right</u> of the clef and the key signature.

3) It's written using <u>two numbers</u>.

The <u>top number</u> tells you <u>how many beats</u> there are in each bar, e.g. a '2' means two beats in a bar, a '3' means three beats in a bar and so on.

TOP NUMBER goes between the middle line and the top line

BOTTOM NUMBER goes between the middle line and the bottom line

The <u>bottom number</u> tells you <u>how long</u> each beat is (see <u>page 8</u> for names of different notes).

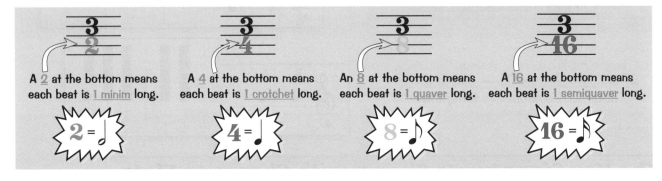

A <u>2</u> at the bottom means each beat is <u>1 minim</u> long.

A <u>4</u> at the bottom means each beat is <u>1 crotchet</u> long.

An <u>8</u> at the bottom means each beat is <u>1 quaver</u> long.

A <u>16</u> at the bottom means each beat is <u>1 semiquaver</u> long.

2 = ♩ 4 = ♩ 8 = ♪ 16 = ♬

If the <u>Beat Changes</u> the <u>Time Signature Changes</u>

1) The time signature usually <u>stays the same</u> all the way through a piece of music. If it does, it's written just <u>once</u>, at the beginning.

2) Sometimes the beat <u>changes</u> during a piece. If it does, the new time signature's written in the bar where it <u>changes</u>.

Not all pieces start on the first beat of the bar — some start on an <u>unaccented beat</u> called an <u>anacrusis</u> (or <u>upbeat</u>).

Music's just like 50s New York — beats everywhere...*

* This is a very <u>pretentious</u> comment, referring to the "Beat Generation" of writers who were around in New York in 1950s. It's so pretentious that I wouldn't be surprised if you <u>ripped this book up</u> in annoyance. But then how would you get through your Music GCSE...

Counting the Beat

Counting the beat's fairly easy, but it's a pretty crucial skill. It'll help you work out how to play a piece you don't know and how to write a tune down when you've only heard it on a CD or in your head.

In Simple Time You Count All the Beats

1) Simple time signatures have 2, 3, or 4 as their top number.

2) In simple time, if you're counting to the music, you count every beat. For $\frac{4}{4}$ you'd count "One, two, three, four." For $\frac{3}{2}$ you'd count "One, two, three."

3) If you want to count out the rhythm of smaller notes as well as the beats, try using "and", "eye" and "a" — it seems to make the rhythm come out just right.

> Count "One and two and" for quavers, and "One eye and a" for semiquavers.

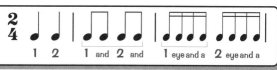

4) Any shorter notes are usually a half, a quarter, an eighth or a sixteenth of the main beat.

In Compound Time Only Count the Big Beats

1) Compound time signatures have 6, 9 or 12 as their top number — you can always divide the top number by three.

2) It's too awkward to count to nine or twelve for every bar. You end up with so many little beats that the rhythm sounds mushy.

3) To make the rhythm clear, every set of three beats is grouped into one:

4) If you were counting out the main beats in $\frac{6}{8}$ you'd count,"One, two. One, two." $\frac{9}{8}$ would go "One, two, three. One, two, three."

5) To count the in-between notes, use "and" and "a".

6) Shorter notes are made by dividing by three — so they're thirds, sixths, twelfths, etc. of the main beat.

7) Music in compound time sounds different from music in simple time — practise spotting the difference.

The Patterns the Beats Make are Called the Metre

Depending on the time signature, the beats make different patterns. The pattern is known as the metre. Metre can be:

REGULAR

The strong beats make the same pattern all the way through.
TWO beats per bar = duple metre
THREE beats per bar = triple metre
FOUR beats per bar = quadruple metre

IRREGULAR

There could be five or seven beats in a bar grouped in twos, threes and fours within each bar.

FREE

Music with no particular metre. This one's fairly unusual.

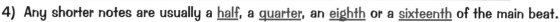

You can describe a time signature based on its beat and metre — e.g. a piece in $\frac{4}{4}$ is in simple quadruple time, and a piece in $\frac{6}{8}$ is in compound duple time.

Zzzzzzzzzzzzzzzzzzzzzzzzzzzzzzzzzzzzzzzzzzzzzzzzzzz...

What?! Oh, sorry. Thought you said counting sheep. Anyway, counting the beat's not really that hard. The tricky bit on this page is the stuff about metre. You could get asked what kind of metre something's in as part of your listening exam so learn all three sorts. And give me back my duvet.

Note & Rest Symbols

Let's face it, you'd be a bit lost reading music if you didn't know what all those funny little dots and squiggles meant. Make sure you know all this stuff better than the alphabet.

The Symbols Tell You How Long Notes and Rests Are

1) Note symbols tell you how many beats to hold a sound for.

2) Rest symbols tell you how many beats to hold a silence for.

3) Notes and rests have names, depending on how long they are.
   For example, two beats is a minim note or rest. A half-beat is a quaver note or rest.

Learn this table now — you need to know exactly how to write these out, and how to play them.

NAME OF NOTE	NUMBER OF CROTCHET BEATS	NOTE SYMBOL	REST SYMBOL
semibreve	4	o	
minim	2		
crotchet	1		
quaver	½	♪ or ♫ ...if there's 2 or more.	
semiquaver	¼	♬ or ♬ ...if there's 2 or more.	

Make sure you know your note lengths.

The Position of the Note Tells You the Pitch

Just in case you don't know one clef from another, this is where the notes go in the bass and treble clefs.

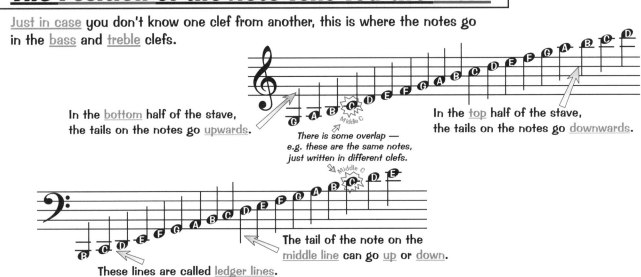

In the bottom half of the stave, the tails on the notes go upwards.

There is some overlap — e.g. these are the same notes, just written in different clefs.

In the top half of the stave, the tails on the notes go downwards.

The tail of the note on the middle line can go up or down.

These lines are called ledger lines. You use them to work out how high or low notes above and below the stave are.

Take note — there is no excuse for not knowing this stuff...

Those of you who were playing the church organ before you could crawl might be feeling a bit like you know this stuff already and you don't need to be told. Well, just check you do know it. Pride comes before a fall, as the revision guide writer said to the...AAAAGH!

Dots, Ties & Triplets

You can only get so far with the note lengths from page 8. If you use dot, tie and triplet symbols you can get more complicated, interesting and sophisticated rhythms. Leading to much wackiness and mirth.

A Dot After a Note or Rest Makes it Longer

1) A dot just to the right of a note or rest makes it half as long again.

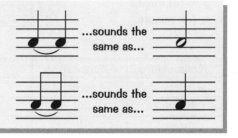

2) A second dot adds on another quarter of the original note length.

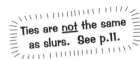

3) Count these really carefully when you're playing — don't just "add a bit on".

A Tie Joins Two Notes Together

1) A tie is a curved line joining two notes of the same pitch together.

2) It turns them into one note.

3) Ties are often used to make a long note that goes over the end of a bar.

...sounds the same as...

...sounds the same as...

Ties are not the same as slurs. See p.11.

A Triplet is Three Notes Played in the Time of Two

1) A triplet is three notes, all the same length, squeezed into the time of two.

2) Triplets are marked with a '3' above or below the middle of the three notes.

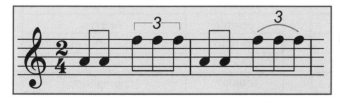

3) Sometimes there's a square bracket or a curved line as well as the three.

4) The notes don't all have to be played — part of a triplet can be rests.

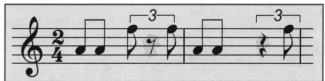

A piglet is one small pig in the space of one small pig...

Triplets. Grrrr. Bane of my life (well, one of them anyway). They look so straightforward on the page, then I try playing them and my fingers get tangled up, my head starts spinning... The only way to get on top of playing them is with a metronome. Boring but true.

Tempo & Mood

Composers are <u>control freaks</u>. They don't just tell you the notes — they tell you <u>how fast</u> to play them, and what the <u>atmosphere</u> of the piece should be too. <u>Get your own back</u> with your own compositions.

The Tempo is the Speed of the Beats

Tempo is Italian for "<u>time</u>". In a lot of music the instructions for how fast to play are written in Italian too. Here are the words you're <u>most</u> likely to come across:

Italian Word	...what it means...	Beats per Minute
largo	broad and slow	40 - 60
larghetto	still broad, not so slow	60 - 66
adagio	bit faster than largo	66 - 76
andante	walking pace	76 - 108
moderato	moderate speed	108 - 120
allegro	quick and lively	120 - 168
vivace	very lively — quicker than allegro	168 - 180
presto	really fast	180 - 200

<u>60</u> beats a minute means each crotchet lasts <u>one second</u>. <u>120</u> beats a minute means each crotchet lasts <u>half a second</u>. And so on...

This is where you put the <u>tempo</u> and <u>beats per minute</u> on the stave. ♩ = 110 means there are 110 crotchet beats per minute. This is called a <u>metronome marking</u>.

Moderato (♩ = 110)

This lot tell you how to <u>vary</u> the speed. The <u>words</u> go <u>underneath</u> the stave. The <u>pause</u> symbol goes <u>above</u>.

Italian Word	Abbreviation	...what it means...
accelerando	accel.	speeding up
rallentando	rall.	slowing down
ritenuto	rit.	holding back the pace
allargando	allarg.	getting slower and broader
rubato	rub.	can be flexible with pace of music
𝄐		pause — longer than a whole beat
a tempo		back to the original pace

Rubato means 'robbed time' — you can <u>slow</u> some bits down and <u>speed</u> others up.

Mood Is the Overall Feel of a Piece

Just for kicks, <u>mood</u>'s usually described in Italian too.

Italian Word	...what it means...
agitato	agitated
alla marcia	in a march style
amoroso	loving
calmato	calm
dolce	soft and sweet
energico	energetic

Italian Word	...what it means...
giocoso	playful, humorous
grandioso	grandly
pesante	heavy
risoluto	strong, confident, bold
sospirando	sighing
trionfale	triumphant

To describe the <u>overall mood</u> put the word at the beginning of the piece.

Andante grandioso (♩=100)
ff

To describe a <u>change of mood</u> write the word under the stave.

p
giocoso

Sometimes parts are marked <u>obbligato</u>, which means they are <u>really important</u> and can't be missed out (*obbligato* means 'obligatory').

WHAT DO YOU MEAN, I'M "IN A MOOD"?!?...

When you're learning the Italian words, start with all the ones that sound a bit like English — they're easy. Once you've learnt them, cross them off. You'll find you've got a much <u>shorter</u> list to learn. Crafty, eh...

Dynamics & Articulation

More cunning little devices for ensnaring players into playing your music <u>exactly</u> how you want it to sound.

Dynamic Markings Tell You How Loud or Quietly to Play

Music that's all played at the <u>same volume</u> would be pretty dull.
To get a <u>variety</u> of different volumes you can use these symbols:

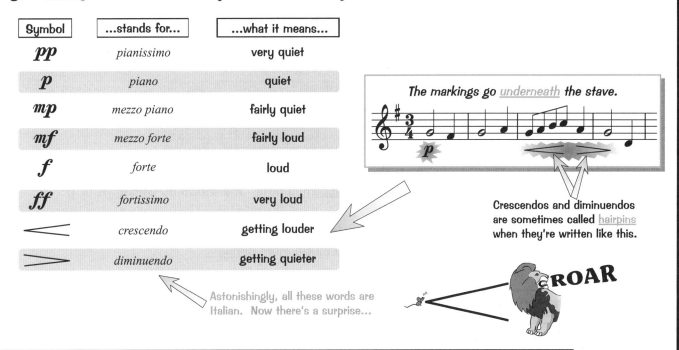

Symbol	...stands for...	...what it means...
pp	*pianissimo*	very quiet
p	*piano*	quiet
mp	*mezzo piano*	fairly quiet
mf	*mezzo forte*	fairly loud
f	*forte*	loud
ff	*fortissimo*	very loud
<	*crescendo*	getting louder
>	*diminuendo*	getting quieter

The markings go <u>underneath</u> the stave.

Crescendos and diminuendos are sometimes called <u>hairpins</u> when they're written like this.

Astonishingly, all these words are Italian. Now there's a surprise...

ROAR

Articulation Tells You How Much to Separate Notes

In theory all the notes of a bar should add up to one <u>continuous</u> sound — but actually there are <u>tiny gaps</u> between them. If you <u>exaggerate</u> the gaps you get a <u>staccato</u> effect. If you smooth the gaps out, the notes sound <u>slurred</u>.

STACCATO — All the dotted notes are played slightly short.

SLUR — All the notes below or above the slur are played smoothly (legato), with no breaks between them.

If the articulation goes <u>all the way through</u> a piece, there's an overall instruction at the <u>beginning</u>.
(If it was to be played smoothly, the instruction would be "<u>legato</u>" here.)

Staccato

Nothing to do with articulated lorries then...

Don't just learn the symbols. Learn what they're <u>called</u> too — it'll sound way, way more impressive if you write about the "<u>dynamics</u>" in your listening exam than if you talk about the "<u>loudness and quietness</u>". Not that you'd do that of course. But I know people who would.

More Instructions

Once a composer has told you how <u>fast</u> and how <u>loud</u> to play and how to <u>articulate</u> it, they sometimes put in <u>extra instructions</u>. Things like <u>accents</u>, <u>sforzandos</u> and <u>bends</u> make the music more <u>interesting</u>.

An Accent Emphasises a Note

1) An <u>accent</u> is a type of articulation that tells you to <u>emphasise</u> (or <u>stress</u>) a note.

2) On a <u>wind</u> instrument, this is often done by <u>tonguing</u> a note <u>harder</u> than normal.

3) Accents are usually written like this > or like this ∧.

4) If a whole <u>section</u> should be accented, it can be marked '*marcato*' (which means 'marked').

5) A <u>sforzando</u> is a <u>strongly accented</u> note. It's shown by writing *sfz* or *sf* underneath the note.

6) A sforzando is often a <u>sudden</u> accent — e.g. a <u>very loud</u> note in a <u>quiet section</u> of a piece. This makes the music more <u>dramatic</u>.

A Glissando is a Slide Between Notes

1) A <u>glissando</u> is a <u>slide</u> from one note to another. Usually you'll be <u>told</u> which notes to <u>start</u> and <u>finish</u> on.

2) A glissando can be played <u>effectively</u> on a <u>violin</u> (or other <u>string</u> instrument), <u>piano</u>, <u>harp</u>, <u>xylophone</u> (or similar instrument), <u>timpani</u> and <u>trombone</u>. Other instruments can play them too, but they often <u>won't</u> sound as <u>good</u>.

3) On some instruments (e.g. piano, harp and xylophone), <u>every note</u> is played in the glissando. Think about it — if you were to play a glissando on a xylophone, you'd run your beater over every note, so they'd all be played.

4) On other instruments, like the trombone and strings, the notes you hear <u>aren't fixed notes</u> — the glissando covers all the <u>tiny differences</u> in pitch between the two notes. For example, you <u>can't</u> pick out <u>individual notes</u> in a glissando on the trombone.

5) A glissando can be shown by writing *gliss.* underneath the stave, or by putting a <u>line</u> between <u>two notes</u>.

Notes can be Bent

1) A <u>bend</u> (or <u>bent note</u>) changes the <u>pitch</u> of the note slightly — it sounds a bit like a <u>wobble</u>.

2) They're often played by starting just <u>above</u> or <u>below</u> the note then <u>bending</u> to it.

3) Bends are often used in <u>jazz music</u>.

4) Bent notes can be played on <u>most</u> instruments — including <u>guitars</u>, <u>trumpets</u>, <u>trombones</u> and <u>harmonicas</u>. <u>Singers</u> can bend notes too.

Roundabouts, swings, climbing frames, glissandi...

All the things on this page are little <u>extras</u> composers can add to their music to make it more <u>interesting</u>. Accented notes and sforzando notes are quite <u>similar</u>, but sforzando notes are usually more <u>unexpected</u>.

Ornaments

Ornaments are fiddly little notes that stand out a bit from the main tune. There are standard symbols used to show all the main ornaments — but there's no standard way of playing them. It's up to the performer.

A Trill is Lots of Tiny Quick Notes

1) If you see the symbol "𝑡𝑟", you play a trill.

2) If the music was written before 1800(ish) start one note above the written note then go quickly back and forth between the written note and the note you started on.

3) If the music was written after 1800(ish) start on the written note and trill up to the note above.

4) The second last note is usually the one below the written note.

5) A sharp, flat or natural sign above the trill symbol tells you if the note to trill to is sharp, flat or natural.

This is how you play the trill if the music's written after 1800. See p.28.

The trill lasts the same length of time as the written note.

An Appoggiatura is an Extra Note in a Chord

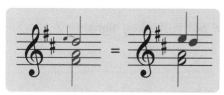

1) The appoggiatura starts on a note that clashes with the chord, then moves to a note that belongs in the chord.

2) The two notes are usually just one tone or semitone apart.

3) It normally takes half the time value of the note it 'leans' on.

4) Appoggiaturas are also called grace notes.

More about appoggiaturas on p.28.

An Acciaccatura is a Tiny Note Squeezed In

An acciaccatura is another type of grace note. It's a note that's squeezed in before the main note and played as fast as possible. "Acciaccatura" means crushing in.

Mordents and Turns are Set Patterns of Notes

MORDENTS

Mordents start off like trills, but the note they end on (the written note) is played a bit longer than the trilled notes.
There are loads of different mordents, but these two are the most common.

upper mordent

lower mordent

TURNS

Start on the note above the written note, then play the written note, followed by the note below the written note. End back on the written note.

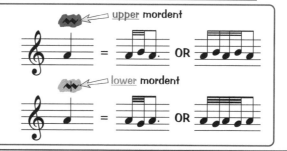

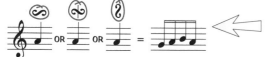

For an inverted turn play the note below the written note, the written note, the note above that, and finally the written note.

China dogs, Spanish dancers, crystal swans and mordents...

The ornaments on this page are "standard" ones, mostly worked out in the 17th century. They still get used nowadays. Jazz players use loads of ornaments too, but they make their own up. That's jazz, baby...

Revision Summary

You'll find a great wodge of questions like this at the end of every section. They're NOT here just to fill up space — they're here to <u>help you</u> test yourself. The basic idea is, if you can answer all the Revision Summary questions and stay as cool as a cucumber, you can be pretty darn sure you've understood and remembered all the important stuff. Look back through the section the first and second time you try the questions, but by the third time you do them, you should be aiming to get <u>all the answers right without looking</u>. I'm serious. Get on with it.

1) Does a clef tell you:
   a) how wide the stave is   b) what instrument it's for   or   c) how high or low the notes on it are?

2) Name two instruments that play music from the bass clef.

3) What's the difference between the symbol for a treble clef and the symbol for the vocal tenor clef?

4) What <u>two</u> other names does the C clef go by?

5) Draw staves showing the C clef in both positions and write the correct name by each one.

6) Draw a sharp sign, a flat sign and a natural sign.

7) What does a sharp do to a note? What does a flat do to a note?

8) Draw each of these signs and explain what you do if you see them by a note:
   a) a double sharp   b) a double flat

9) Draw a treble clef stave and add a key signature with one sharp.

10) What do you call a sharp, flat or natural sign when it's in the music but not in the key signature?

11) One beat in the bar usually feels stronger than the others. Which one?

12) What do you call the two numbers at the start of a piece of music?

13) What does the top number tell you about the beats? What does the bottom number tell you?

14) When a time signature changes in a piece of music, where's the new one written?

15) What's another name for an upbeat?

16) What's the difference between simple and compound time?

17) What's the difference between regular and irregular metre?

18) Give an example of a time signature that could be described as compound duple time.

19) Draw the symbol for each of the following notes and write down how many crotchet beats it lasts:
   a) semibreve   b) minim   c) crotchet   d) quaver   e) semiquaver

20) Draw a stave with a treble clef at the beginning. Draw on middle C and mark on 16 letter names above it.

21) Draw a stave with a bass clef at the beginning. Draw on middle C and mark on 16 letter names below it.

22) What does a dot immediately after a note or rest do?

23) What's the time value of:
   a) a dotted crotchet   b) a dotted minim   c) a double dotted minim?

24) What does a 'tie' do?

25) How much time, in crotchet beats, does a crotchet triplet take up?

26) Which is slower, *allegro* or *moderato*?

27) Where do you put the tempo marking on a stave?

28) What does *dolce* mean?

29) How do composers show on the written music that they want the notes to be played smoothly?

30) How are accents usually indicated in a piece of music?

31) What's a glissando?

32) Describe an appoggiatura.

33) What are the notes of an upper mordent starting on F?

34) What are the notes of an inverted turn starting on C?

Major Scales

There are two main types of scales — major and minor. Once you know how scales are put together, keys and chords make lots more sense. Honest.

Ordinary Scales have Eight Notes

The gap between the bottom and top notes of a scale is called an octave. See p.19.

1) An ordinary major or minor scale has 8 notes, starting and ending on notes of the same name, e.g. C major goes C, D, E, F, G, A, B, C.

2) Each of the eight notes has a name.

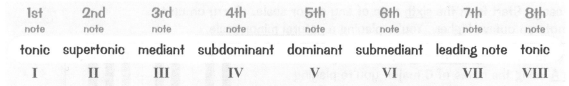

1st note	2nd note	3rd note	4th note	5th note	6th note	7th note	8th note
tonic	supertonic	mediant	subdominant	dominant	submediant	leading note	tonic
I	II	III	IV	V	VI	VII	VIII

3) You can just use the numbers or the Roman numerals to name the notes too.

Major Scales Sound Bright and Cheery

Whatever note they start on, all major scales sound similar, because they all follow the same pattern. The pattern's a set order of tone and semitone gaps between the notes:

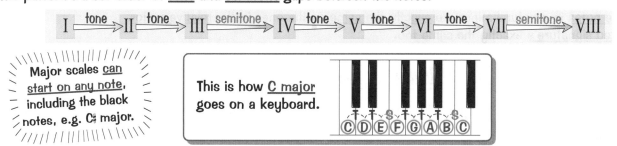

$$I \xrightarrow{\text{tone}} II \xrightarrow{\text{tone}} III \xrightarrow{\text{semitone}} IV \xrightarrow{\text{tone}} V \xrightarrow{\text{tone}} VI \xrightarrow{\text{tone}} VII \xrightarrow{\text{semitone}} VIII$$

Major scales can start on any note, including the black notes, e.g. C♯ major.

This is how C major goes on a keyboard.

All Major Scales except C have One or More Black Notes

C major is the only major scale with no black notes.
All the others need at least one black note to stick to the 'tone-semitone' pattern.

1) G major scale — you have to change F to F♯ to make the notes fit the major scale pattern.

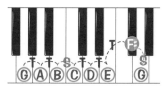

2) F major scale — you have to change B to B♭ to make the pattern right.

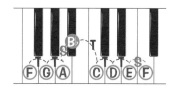

The Set of Notes in a Scale is called a Key

1) The key tells you what sharps and flats there are (if any) in a piece.

2) To show what key the piece is in, a sharp or flat sign goes on the stave at the start (before the time signature) for every sharp or flat note in the scale. This is called the KEY SIGNATURE.

3) A key signature can have sharps or flats but NEVER both.

4) If a piece changes key, it's called a modulation — see p.31.

The key signature goes in between the clef and the time signature.

G major's got one sharp note — F♯. You put a sharp symbol on the F line.

Major Scales — a fine officer, though somewhat flaky...

Try playing some major scales starting on different notes. Even if you don't "know" them, you should be able to work out what the notes are, using the tone-semitone pattern and the sound. If you can work out any scale that means you can easily work out any key too — two gems of knowledge for the price of one.

Minor Scales

Minor scales have fixed patterns too. Unfortunately, there are <u>three</u> different kinds you need to know.

Minor Scales All Sound a Bit Mournful

Minor scales sound <u>completely different</u> from major scales, because they've got a different tone-semitone pattern. There are <u>three</u> types of minor scale, and all of them sound a bit <u>sad</u>.

1) The Natural Minor Uses All the Same Notes as the Relative Major

These are easy. Start from the <u>sixth</u> note of any major scale. Carry on up to the same note an octave higher. You're playing a <u>natural minor scale</u>.

The sixth note of <u>C major</u> is <u>A</u>. If you play from <u>A to A</u> using the notes of C major, you're playing <u>A natural minor</u> (usually just called '<u>A minor</u>').

PAIRS OF KEYS LIKE <u>A MINOR AND C MAJOR</u> ARE CALLED "<u>RELATIVE</u>" KEYS.
A MINOR IS THE <u>RELATIVE MINOR</u> OF C MAJOR.
C MAJOR IS THE <u>RELATIVE MAJOR</u> OF A MINOR.

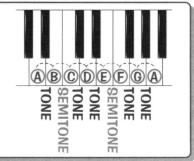

<u>All the notes</u> in a natural minor are <u>exactly the same</u> as the ones in the <u>relative major</u>. The <u>key signature's</u> exactly the same too.

2) The Harmonic Minor has One Accidental

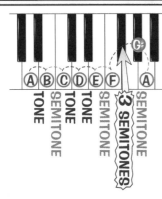

1) The <u>harmonic minor</u> has the same notes as the relative major, except for the <u>seventh note</u>.

2) The <u>seventh</u> note is always raised by <u>one semitone</u>.

3) You use the harmonic minor when you're writing <u>harmonies</u>. That <u>sharpened seventh note</u> makes the harmonies work much better than they would with notes from a natural minor. It's probably because it sort of feels like it wants to move up to the tonic.

3) The Melodic Minor has Two Accidentals to Make it More Tuneful

1) The <u>melodic minor</u> is just like a natural minor, using the notes from the relative major scale, <u>except for notes 6 and 7</u>.

2) On the way <u>up</u>, notes <u>6</u> and <u>7</u> are each <u>raised</u> by <u>one semitone</u>.

3) On the way <u>down</u>, the melodic minor goes just like the natural minor.

4) The melodic minor is used for writing <u>melodies</u>. Those two accidentals make tunes sound <u>smoother</u> by avoiding the big jump between notes 6 and 7 in the harmonic minor.

And not forgetting the Morris Minor...

Three minor scales... couldn't they have stopped at two... You really do need to learn <u>all three</u> — names, notes, how they relate to the relative major, and what they're used for. They're really useful if you're writing a piece that's meant to be <u>sad</u> — they all sound a bit <u>melancholy</u> and <u>miserable</u>.

The Circle of Fifths

The circle of fifths is a bit mad-professorish, but very useful — it tells you all the keys, all the relative keys and their key signatures.

The Circle of Fifths Shows All the Keys

1) Altogether there are 12 major keys. They're all shown on the circle of fifths.
2) Don't expect to fully get it if this is the first time you've seen it. Just have a look then read on.

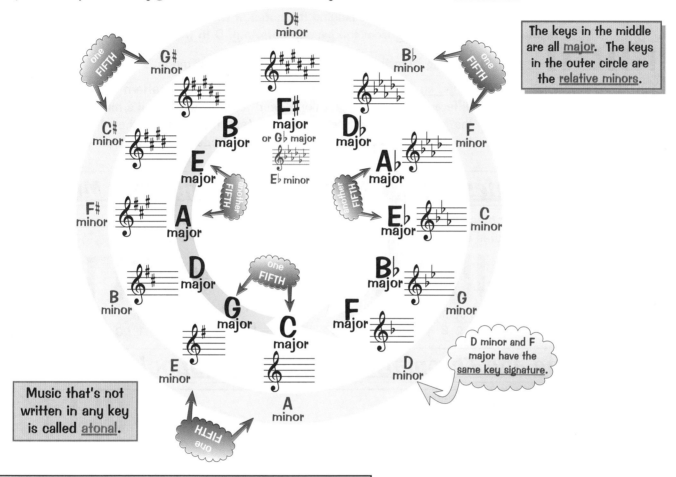

The keys in the middle are all major. The keys in the outer circle are the relative minors.

Music that's not written in any key is called atonal.

D minor and F major have the same key signature.

Each Key Links to the Next One

1) The circle starts with C major at the bottom. The next key round is G. G's the fifth note of C major.
2) The fifth note of G major is D, the next key on the circle. This pattern repeats all the way round. That's why the chart's called the circle of fifths.
3) As you go round the circle the number of sharps in the key signature goes up one for each key.
4) When you get to F♯ major at the top there are six sharps. From here, you start writing the key signature in flats — you don't need as many so it's clearer to read.
5) The number of flats keeps going down until you get back to C major, with no sharps and no flats.
6) The relative minors in the outer circle work just the same way as the major keys — the fifth note of A minor is E and the next minor key's E minor... and so on. Don't forget you can always work out the relative minor by counting up to the sixth note of a major scale, (see p.16) or the relative major by counting up to the third note of the minor scale.

This is making my head spin...

In one way the circle of fifths is very simple. Then if you think about it too much it turns into a total mind-frier. Memorise it if you want, but you're better off remembering how it works, then you can always work out what you need to know.

Modes & Other Types of Scales

There are a few <u>weirdy scales</u> that you need to know about. And <u>modes</u>. They're very odd.

Modes *Follow* Different Patterns *of Tones* and *Semitones*

<u>Modes</u> are just like playing the notes of a <u>scale</u>, but starting on <u>different notes</u>.

1) The most <u>common</u> mode is the one you get by playing a <u>major scale</u> (e.g. C major — just play the <u>white</u> notes on a keyboard from C to C). The pattern is *tone-tone-semitone-tone-tone-tone-semitone*.

2) Another mode can be formed by playing the notes of the same major scale, starting from the <u>second note</u>, e.g. D to D:

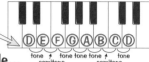

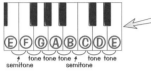

3) Starting from the third note gives you another mode...

This one sounds a bit Spanish — it's used a lot in flamenco music.

4) ...<u>and so on</u>. Each forms its own semitone / tone pattern and they all have different names, but you don't need to know them — it's more important that you <u>know what they sound like</u> (e.g. it's handy to know that playing the white notes starting from G forms a mode that sounds quite bluesy).

Pentatonic *Scales are Used a lot in* Folk *and* Rock Music

Pentatonic scales use <u>five</u> notes. They're really easy to compose with, because there are <u>no semitone steps</u> — <u>most combinations</u> of notes sound fine. There are <u>two types</u> of pentatonic scale.

1) The <u>major pentatonic</u> uses notes 1, 2, 3, 5 and 6 of a <u>major</u> scale.

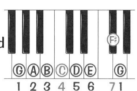

2) The <u>minor pentatonic</u> uses notes 1, 3, 4, 5 and 7 of the <u>natural minor</u> scale.

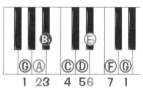

Whole Tone *and* Chromatic Scales *Sound Spooky*

WHOLE TONE SCALES

Whole tone scales are pretty simple to remember — <u>every step is a tone</u>. From bottom to top there are only <u>seven notes</u> in a whole tone scale.

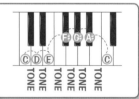

Major and minor scales are known as <u>diatonic scales</u>.

CHROMATIC SCALES

Chromatic scales are fairly easy too. On a keyboard you play <u>every white and black note</u> until you get up to an octave above the note you started with. From bottom to top there are <u>thirteen notes</u>. Basically <u>every step</u> of a chromatic scale is <u>a semitone</u>.

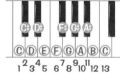

Blues has its Own Scale

1) You get a blues scale by <u>flattening</u> the <u>third</u> and <u>seventh</u> of any major scale by a semitone. The <u>fifth</u> note's sometimes flattened too.

2) The flattened notes are known as the <u>blue notes</u>.

3) The <u>second</u> and <u>sixth</u> notes are often left out.

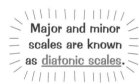

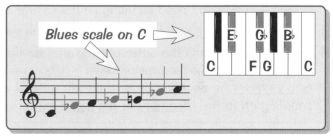

Blues scale on C

I'd like a pentatonic with ice and a slice...

You <u>could</u> get a piece of music in your <u>listening exam</u> that's written in a <u>mode</u> or one of the other <u>scales</u>. And you could get <u>asked</u> what kind of scale it's written with — so make sure you know them.

Intervals

No — not the break at half-time when everyone rushes out for an <u>ice-cream</u>. The musical kind.

An <u>Interval</u> is the <u>Gap</u> Between <u>Two Notes</u>

An interval is the posh <u>musical word</u> for the <u>gap</u> or <u>distance</u> between <u>two notes</u>.
Notes <u>close together</u> make <u>small</u> intervals. Notes <u>further apart</u> make <u>larger</u> intervals.
There are <u>two ways</u> of playing an interval.

MELODIC INTERVAL
When one note <u>jumps</u> up or down to another note, you get a <u>melodic interval</u>.

ASCENDING interval   DESCENDING interval

HARMONIC INTERVAL
When <u>two notes</u> are played at the <u>same time</u>, they make a <u>harmonic interval</u>.

1) You can use the <u>melodic intervals</u> to describe the <u>pattern</u> of a <u>melody</u>.
2) In some melodies, there are only <u>small</u> intervals between the notes — no bigger than a <u>tone</u>.
3) When the notes are <u>close together</u> like this, the melody can be called <u>stepwise</u>, <u>conjunct</u> or <u>scalic</u> (because it moves up and down the notes of a <u>scale</u>).
4) Tunes with <u>big</u> melodic intervals (larger than a tone) are called <u>disjunct</u>.

An <u>Interval</u> has <u>Two Parts</u> to its Name...

1) A <u>NUMBER</u>
an augmented fifth
2) A <u>DESCRIPTION</u>

The <u>Number</u> Tells You <u>How Many Notes</u> the Interval Covers

1) You get the number by counting up the stave from the <u>bottom</u> note to the <u>top</u> note. You <u>include</u> the bottom and top notes in your counting.

2) C to E is a <u>third</u> because it covers <u>three letter names</u> — C, D and E.

3) C to F is a <u>fourth</u> because it covers <u>four letter names</u> — C, D, E and F.

4) The number of an interval is sometimes called the <u>interval quantity</u>.

The "description" bit is covered at the top of the next page...

The interval between G and D is a <u>fifth</u>.
G A B C D
1 2 3 4 5

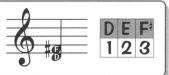

The interval between D and F sharp is a <u>third</u> (you can just <u>ignore</u> the accidentals when counting).
D E F♯
1 2 3

An interval covering <u>eight letters</u> — say A to A — is called an <u>octave</u>. It's just got one name — it doesn't follow the two-part name rule.

Intervals

The Description Tells You How the Interval Sounds

There are five names for the five main sounds:

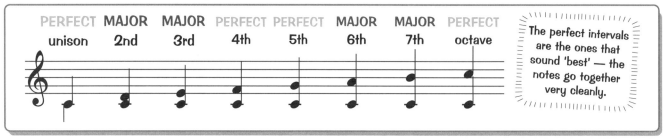

perfect   major   minor   diminished   augmented

1) To work out the description part of an interval's name, think of the lower note of the interval as the first note of a major scale.

2) If the top note of the interval is part of that major scale it's either perfect or major:

PERFECT	MAJOR	MAJOR	PERFECT	PERFECT	MAJOR	MAJOR	PERFECT
unison	2nd	3rd	4th	5th	6th	7th	octave

The perfect intervals are the ones that sound 'best' — the notes go together very cleanly.

3) If the top note doesn't belong to the major scale, then it's minor, diminished or augmented.

> If the interval is one semitone LESS than a major interval, then it's MINOR.
> If the interval is one semitone LESS than a minor or a perfect interval, then it's DIMINISHED.
> If the interval is one semitone MORE than a major or a perfect interval, then it's AUGMENTED.

Work Out the Full Name of an Interval Step by Step

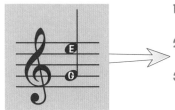

1. HOW MANY LETTER NAMES DOES IT COVER?
   Six — G, A, B, C, D and E. So the quantity's a sixth.
2. ARE THE NOTES FROM THE SAME MAJOR SCALE?
   The bottom note's G. E is in G major — it's the sixth note.
3. WHAT TYPE OF INTERVAL IS IT?
   It's the sixth note of G major, and the sixth note always gives a major interval — so it's a MAJOR SIXTH.

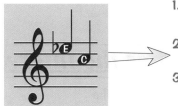

1. HOW MANY LETTER NAMES DOES IT COVER?
   Three — C, D and E♭. So the quantity's a third.
2. ARE THE NOTES FROM THE SAME MAJOR SCALE?
   Nope.
3. WHAT TYPE OF INTERVAL IS IT?
   The third note of C major is E, so a major third would be C to E. This interval's one semitone smaller, so it's a MINOR THIRD.

The Tritone Interval Sounds Odd

1) The tritone is an interval of three tones. It's dissonant — i.e. it sounds a bit awkward, some would say horrible. It's used in some twentieth century Western art music.

2) Diminished fifths (e.g. G to D♭) and augmented fourths (e.g. G to C♯) are both tritones.

3) Try playing some, so you know what they sound like.

Have you got an interval or an outerval...

The tritone interval used to be called 'The Devil's Interval' — it's supposed to be unlucky.
It's used somewhere in the Blackadder theme tune actually. Kinda appropriate I guess.

Revision Summary

I hope you're hungry — I've got some delicious Revision Summary questions for you, fresh out of the oven. Once you've got on top of these, you can sit back and feel smug. But only when you can answer them <u>without</u> looking back at the section...

1) How many notes are there in a major scale?

2) Write out the names of the notes of a scale in words, numbers and Roman numerals.

3) Write down the tone-semitone pattern for a major scale.

4) Which major scale only uses the white notes on the keyboard?

5) Why do all the other major scales have black notes?

6) What does a key signature tell you?

7) What's wrong with this key signature?

8) How do you find the 'relative minor' of a major scale?

9) How do you find the 'relative major' of a minor scale?

10) D major has two sharps — F and C. What's the key signature of the relative minor?

11) What are the three different types of minor scale called?

12) Write out A minor in each of the three types of minor scale and label the tone and semitone gaps.

13) How many major scales are there altogether? How many minor scales are there altogether?

14) The circle of fifths starts with C major. Write down all the major scales on the circle, in order, starting with C.

15) What's the name given to music that's not written in any key?

16) Write out two common modes.

17) What's a pentatonic scale? What types of music do you find pentatonic scales in a lot?

18) What are the notes in G major pentatonic?

19) What are the notes in A minor pentatonic?

20) What's a whole tone scale?

21) What's a chromatic scale? How many notes are there in a chromatic scale?

22) What are diatonic scales?

23) Which notes are flattened in a blues scale?

24) What's the difference between a melodic and a harmonic interval?

25) What is a stepwise tune?

26) Give the description and number of each of these intervals:

   a) A to C

   b) B to F♯

   c) C to B♭

   d) D to A♭

27) What's a tritone?

Chords — The Basics

A <u>chord</u> is at least two notes played together. Chords are great for writing <u>accompaniments</u>.
In fact, no chords, no accompaniments.

Only Some Instruments Play Chords

Don't play chords.

Do play chords.

1) A lot of instruments only play <u>one note at a time</u> — flutes, recorders, trumpets, clarinets, trombones... You can't play a chord with one note, so these instruments <u>don't</u> play chords.

2) You can <u>only</u> play chords on <u>instruments</u> that play <u>more than one</u> note at a time. <u>Keyboards</u> and <u>guitars</u> are both great for playing chords — you can easily play several notes together.

3) Other <u>stringed instruments</u> like violins and cellos can play chords, but <u>not</u> very easily, so chords are only played from time to time.

Some Chords Sound Great, Others Sound Awful

1) The notes of some chords go together really well — like apple pie and ice-cream.

2) Other chords have <u>clashing notes</u> <u>which disagree</u> — more like apple pie and pickled eggs.

> When you have nice-sounding chords it's called <u>CONCORDANCE</u> or <u>CONSONANCE</u>.

> When you have horrible-sounding chords it's called <u>DISCORDANCE</u> or <u>DISSONANCE</u>.

The Best-Sounding Chords are Called Triads

1) You can play <u>any</u> set of notes and make a chord — but most of them sound <u>awful</u>.

2) An <u>easy</u>, <u>reliable</u> way of getting nice-sounding chords is to play <u>triads</u>.

3) Triads are chords made up of <u>three notes</u>, with <u>set intervals</u> between them.

4) Once you know the intervals, you can easily play <u>dozens</u> of decent chords.

HOW TO MAKE A TRIAD...

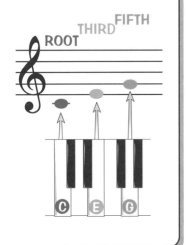

ROOT THIRD FIFTH

1) On a piano, start with any white note — this is called the <u>root note</u>. You <u>build</u> the triad <u>from the root</u>.

2) Count the root as 'first' and the next white note to the <u>right</u>, as 'second'. The <u>third</u> note you reach is the <u>third</u> — the middle note of the triad.

3) Keep counting up and you get to the <u>fifth</u> — the final note of the triad.

4) The intervals between the notes are <u>thirds</u>.

5) If the root note's a <u>B</u>, then you end up with a <u>B triad</u>. If the root note's a <u>C</u>, you end up with a <u>C triad</u>.

6) You can build triads on black notes too, so long as the intervals between notes are <u>thirds</u>.

Chords — your music teacher's favourite trousers...

This looks like another of those pages where you might know it all already. Still, it won't hurt to read through again and <u>check</u> you <u>really do</u> know it all. The rest of this section gets tricky so enjoy the easy stuff while it lasts...

Triads

There's more than one type of triad...

Triads Use Major and Minor Thirds

1) All triads have an interval of a <u>third</u> between each pair of notes.

2) The intervals can be <u>major</u> or <u>minor thirds</u>.

A <u>major third</u> is <u>four</u> semitones.

A <u>minor third</u> is <u>three</u> semitones.

3) Different <u>combinations</u> of major and minor thirds give different types of triad:

MAJOR TRIADS

- <u>Major triads</u> have a <u>major third</u> followed by a <u>minor third</u>.
- The <u>major third</u> goes between the root and the third.
- The <u>minor third</u> goes between the third and the fifth.

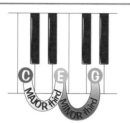

MINOR TRIADS

- <u>Minor triads</u> use a <u>major</u> and a <u>minor third</u> too, but in the opposite order.
- The <u>minor third</u> goes between the root and the third.
- The <u>major third</u> goes between the third and the fifth.

DIMINISHED TRIADS use <u>two minor thirds</u>.
AUGMENTED TRIADS use <u>two major thirds</u>.

These two kinds aren't nearly as common as major and minor triads.

You Can Add a Note to a Triad to Get a 7th Chord

1) <u>7th chords</u> are triads with a fourth note added — the <u>seventh</u> note above the root.

2) The interval between the root and the 7th can be <u>major seventh</u> or a <u>minor seventh</u> — see p.20.

Chords can be Written as Symbols

C = C major	Cm = C minor
Caug or C+ = augmented C chord	Cdim or C- or Co = diminished C chord
C7 = C major with added minor 7th	Cm7 = C minor with added minor 7th
Cmaj7 = C major with added major 7th	Cm maj7 = C minor with added major 7th

For chords other than C just change the <u>first letter</u> to show the <u>root note</u>.

Does this look hard — it's easy when you triad...

Those symbols come up all the time in pop music — if you play the guitar or play in a band you need to learn them <u>right now</u>. And even if you only ever play baroque music on period instruments you'd <u>still</u> better learn 'em — they're really useful as shorthand when you're talking about chords.

Fitting Chords to a Melody

When you're fitting chords to a melody, the notes in the chords have to be in the <u>same key</u> as the melody.

The Melody and Chords Must Be in the Same Key

1) A melody that's composed in a certain key <u>sticks</u> to that key.
2) The chords used to <u>harmonise with</u> the melody have got to be in the <u>same key</u> or it'll sound <u>awful</u>.
3) As a <u>general rule</u> each chord in a <u>simple</u> harmony should <u>include</u> the note it's accompanying,
   e.g. a <u>C</u> could be accompanied by a <u>C chord</u> (C, E, G), an <u>F chord</u> (F, A, C) or an <u>A minor chord</u> (A, C, E).

There's a Chord for Every Note in the Scale

You can make a whole bunch of triads using the notes of <u>major</u> and <u>minor</u> scales as the <u>roots</u>. <u>Every note</u> of <u>every chord</u>, not just the root, has to belong to the scale. This is how <u>C major</u> looks if you turn it into chords:

> The odd accidental or ornament in a different key is OK — see p.28.

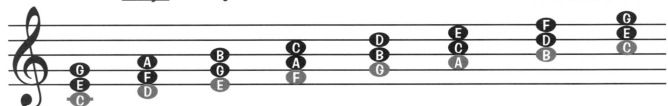

Chord I	Chord II	Chord III	Chord IV	Chord V	Chord VI	Chord VII	Chord I
Tonic	Supertonic	Mediant	Subdominant	Dominant	Submediant	Leading Note	Tonic

1) Chords I, IV and V are <u>major triads</u>. They sound <u>bright and cheery</u>. A <u>7th</u> can be added to <u>chord V</u> to give a <u>dominant 7th</u> chord (written V^7).
2) Chords II, III and VI are <u>minor triads</u>. They sound more <u>gloomy</u>.
3) Chord VII is a <u>diminished triad</u>. It sounds really <u>different</u> from the major and minor chords. Another name for Chord VII is the <u>Leading Note Chord</u> — it sounds a bit like it should lead on to another chord.
4) Chords built on <u>any</u> major scale, not just C major, follow the <u>same pattern</u>.
5) A <u>series</u> of chords is known as a <u>harmonic progression</u> (or <u>chord progression</u>).
6) The <u>speed</u> at which the chords <u>change</u> is called the <u>harmonic rhythm</u>.

The Primary Triads are Most Useful

1) The three major chords, <u>I</u>, <u>IV</u> and <u>V</u>, are the <u>most important</u> in <u>any</u> key. They're called <u>primary triads</u>.
2) Between them, the primary triads can harmonise with <u>any note</u> in the scale.
3) This is how it works in <u>C major</u>:

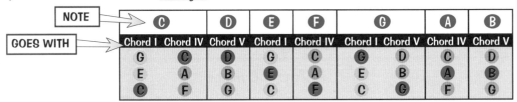

Minor Chords Make Harmony More Interesting

1) Primary chords can get a bit <u>boring</u> to listen to after a while — the harmonies are fairly <u>simple</u>.
2) Composers often mix in a few of the other chords — <u>II</u>, <u>III</u>, <u>VI</u> or <u>VII</u> — for a <u>change</u>.
3) Instead of just having endless major chords, you get a mixture of <u>minor</u> and <u>diminished</u> chords too.

Go on, write a harmony, you know you want to...

Actually, you can't turn <u>any</u> scale into chords. You can't turn a <u>fish scale</u> or a <u>lizard scale</u> into chords. But any major or minor scale you can turn into chords. And once you've done that you can fit them to your melody. Try the major chords first, then liven things up with some minor chords.

Inversions

Inverting triads means changing the order of the notes. It helps make accompaniments a bit more varied.

Triads with the Root at the Bottom are in Root Position

These triads are all in root position — the root note is at the bottom.

- = fifth
- = third
- = root

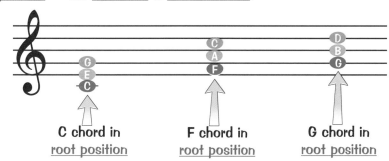

C chord in root position

F chord in root position

G chord in root position

First Inversion Triads have the Third at the Bottom

These chords are all in first inversion. The root note's moved up an octave, leaving the third at the bottom.

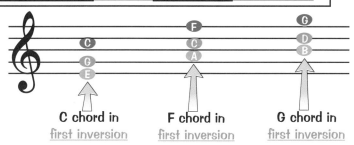

C chord in first inversion

F chord in first inversion

G chord in first inversion

Second Inversion Triads have the Fifth at the Bottom

Chords can be played in second inversion too.

From the first inversion, the third is raised an octave, leaving the fifth at the bottom.

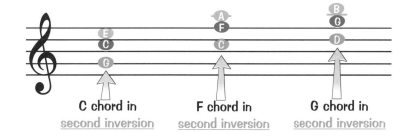

C chord in second inversion

F chord in second inversion

G chord in second inversion

7th Chords can go into a Third Inversion

1) 7th chords can be played in root position, first inversion or second inversion — just like triads.
2) But there's also a third inversion — from the second inversion, the fifth is raised an octave, leaving the seventh at the bottom.

There's a Symbol for each Inversion

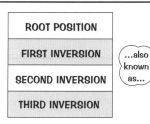
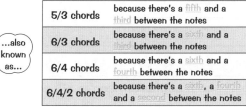

ROOT POSITION	5/3 chords	because there's a fifth and a third between the notes	Ia
FIRST INVERSION	6/3 chords	because there's a sixth and a third between the notes	Ib
SECOND INVERSION	6/4 chords	because there's a sixth and a fourth between the notes	Ic
THIRD INVERSION	6/4/2 chords	because there's a sixth, a fourth and a second between the notes	Id

...also known as... ...and in Roman numerals... ...and in good old chord symbols...

C	a C chord
C/E	a C chord with the E at the bottom
C/G	a C chord with the G at the bottom
Cmaj7/B	a C 7th chord with the B at the bottom

Inversions

So now you know what inversions <u>are</u>, it's time to get to grips with what to <u>do</u> with them too...

Inversions <u>are Handy</u> for *Moving Between Chords*

When you play chords one after another, it sounds <u>nicer</u> if the notes move <u>smoothly</u> from one chord to the next. Inversions help to smooth out any rough patches...

1) Moving from a <u>C chord in root position</u> to a <u>G chord in root position</u> means <u>all</u> the notes have to jump <u>a long way</u>. It sounds <u>clumsy</u> and not all that nice.

● = fifth
● = third
● = root

2) If you move from a C chord in root position to a <u>G chord</u> in <u>first inversion</u> instead, the transition is much, much smoother.

Try playing both sets of chords a few times, until you can hear the difference.

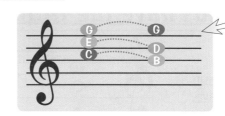

3) You can use <u>second</u> and <u>third inversions</u> too — whatever sounds best.

Unscramble <u>the Inversion</u> to work out the *Root Note*

This isn't exactly a life-saving skill. But it's <u>dead useful</u>...
If you come across an inverted chord you can <u>work out</u> which is the <u>root note</u>. Once you know that, and you know what <u>key</u> you're in, you can tell whether it's chord **IV**, **VII**, **II** or whatever.

1) Basically you have to turn the chord back into a <u>root position triad</u>.

2) Shuffle the order of the notes around until there's a <u>third interval</u> between each one.

3) When the notes are arranged in <u>thirds</u>, the root will <u>always</u> be at the <u>bottom</u>.

B to D is a **THIRD**, but D to G is a **FOURTH**.
You need to <u>move the G</u> to find the root chord.

G to B is a **THIRD** so the G goes here
— <u>G</u>'s the <u>root note</u>.

4) There are no sharps or flats in the key signature, so the piece is in C major.
G's the fifth note of C major, so this is <u>chord V</u>.

Unscramble inversions — go back to your roots...

Well, if those two pages haven't made your ears <u>bleed</u> with confusion, you're either superhuman, subhuman or a music genius. There's a lot to take in, so go over it one bit at a time till you <u>really</u> get it.

Different Ways of Playing Chords

So far, all the chords in this section have been written as three notes played together. It sounds a bit dull. To make things more interesting composers use <u>chord figurations</u> — different ways of playing the chords.

Block Chords <u>are the Most Basic</u>

This is probably the <u>easiest</u> way to play chords. The notes of each chord are played <u>all together</u> and then <u>held</u> until the next chord.

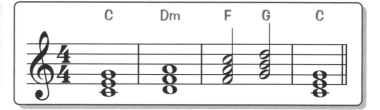

Rhythmic Chords <u>Give You</u> Harmony <u>and Rhythm</u>

1) Rhythmic chords are <u>chords played</u> to a <u>funky rhythm</u>.

2) You play all the notes of each chord at the same time, like you do for block chords.

3) You don't <u>hold</u> the notes though — you play them to a <u>rhythm</u> that <u>repeats</u> in each bar.

4) <u>Rhythm guitar</u> and <u>keyboards</u> often play rhythmic chords.

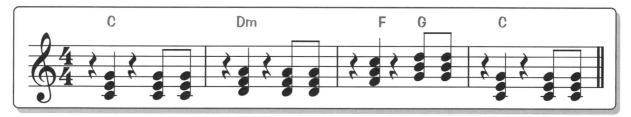

In Broken <u>and</u> Arpeggiated Chords <u>Notes are Separate</u>

An accompaniment <u>doesn't</u> have to have chords with all the notes played at once. You can play the notes <u>separately</u> too.

1) Here's one way of doing it — it goes <u>root</u>, <u>fifth</u>, <u>third</u>, <u>root</u>.

2) This pattern was dead popular around the time <u>Mozart</u> was alive (last half of the 1700s). It's called <u>Alberti bass</u> after the bloke who made it up (Domenico Alberti) — it goes <u>root</u>, <u>fifth</u>, <u>third</u>, <u>fifth</u>.

3) The <u>notes of a chord</u> are sometimes <u>played in order</u> (root, third, fifth, root) <u>going up</u> or <u>coming down</u>. This is called an <u>arpeggio</u> (*are-pej-ee-o*).

4) A <u>walking bass</u> usually moves in <u>crotchets</u>, often either in <u>steps</u> (see p.19) or <u>arpeggios</u>.

5) A <u>drone</u> is a <u>long</u>, <u>held-on note</u>, usually in the <u>bass</u>, that adds harmonic interest.

Alberti's Haddock doesn't have quite the same ring...

You know when you get chord symbols over the music... well, when that happens, it basically means you can play the chords <u>any way you like</u>. Try out all the ways of playing chords on this page and think about <u>using them</u> in your compositions — don't get stuck with boring old block chords.

Using Decoration to Vary the Harmony

If you want to <u>liven things up</u> in a harmony you can add a sprinkle of <u>melodic decoration</u> —
a fancy way of saying <u>bung a few extra notes in</u>.

Melodic Decoration Adds Notes to the Tune

1) <u>Decorative notes</u> are <u>short notes</u> that create <u>fleeting clashes</u> or <u>dissonance</u> with the accompanying chord. They make things sound <u>less bland</u>.

2) Decoration that belongs to the key of the melody (e.g. B in C major) is called <u>DIATONIC</u>.

3) Decoration that <u>doesn't</u> belong to the key (e.g. F♯ in C major) is called <u>CHROMATIC</u>.

4) There are <u>four</u> main ways of adding melodic decoration:

1) Auxiliary Notes are Higher or Lower than the Notes Either Side

1) An auxiliary note is either a <u>semitone</u> or <u>tone</u> <u>above</u> or <u>below</u> the notes either side.

2) The two notes before and after the auxiliary are always the <u>same pitch</u>, and always belong to the accompanying chord.

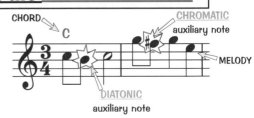

2) Passing Notes Link the Notes

1) A passing note <u>links</u> the notes before and after. Both of them have to belong to the accompanying chord.

2) They're usually put on <u>weak beats</u>. When they're on the <u>strong beat</u> they're called <u>accented passing notes</u>.

3) Appoggiaturas Clash with the Chord

1) An appoggiatura <u>clashes</u> with the accompanying chord.

2) The note <u>before</u> it is usually quite a <u>leap</u> away (jumps between notes of more than a <u>2nd</u> are called <u>leaps</u>).

3) The note <u>after</u> the appoggiatura is always <u>just above</u> or <u>below</u>. It's called the <u>resolution</u>. The <u>resolution</u> has to be from the <u>accompanying chord</u>.

4) Appoggiaturas usually fall on a <u>strong beat</u>, so the resolution note falls on a <u>weaker beat</u>.

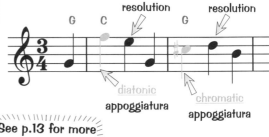

See p.13 for more on appoggiaturas.

4) Suspensions Clash then Go Back to Harmonising

A suspension is a series of three notes called the <u>preparation</u>, <u>suspension</u> and <u>resolution</u>.

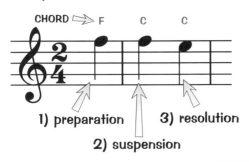

1) The <u>preparation</u> note <u>belongs</u> to the <u>accompanying chord</u>. It's usually on a <u>weak beat</u>.

2) The <u>suspension</u> is the <u>same pitch</u> as the preparation note. It's played at the <u>same time</u> as a <u>chord change</u>. It <u>doesn't go</u> with the new chord, so you get <u>dissonance</u>.

3) The <u>resolution</u> note moves <u>up or down</u> (usually down) from the <u>suspension</u> to a note in the <u>accompanying chord</u>. This <u>resolves</u> the dissonance — everything sounds lovely again.

Passing notes is so juvenile...

The best way to get the hang of melodic decorations is to <u>try them out</u> for yourself when you're composing. And once you've got the hang of them, use them — you're likely to get <u>higher marks</u>.

Phrases and Cadences

Notes in a melody fall into 'phrases' just like the words in a story fall into phrases and sentences. A cadence is the movement from the second-last chord to the last chord of a phrase — to finish the phrase off nicely.

A Phrase is like a Musical Sentence

There should be clear phrases in any melody. A tune without phrases would sound odd — just like a story with no sentences wouldn't make much sense.

1) Phrases are usually two or four bars long.

2) Phrases are sometimes marked with a curved line called a phrase mark, that goes above the stave. Not all music has phrase marks but the phrases are always there. Don't confuse phrase marks and slurs. A phrase mark doesn't change how you play the notes.

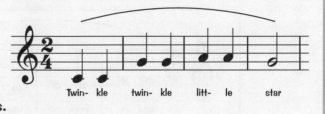

Cadences Emphasise the End of a Phrase

1) A cadence is the shift between the second-last chord and the last chord in a phrase.

2) The effect you get from shifting between the two chords works like a comma or a full stop. It underlines the end of the phrase and gets you ready for the next one.

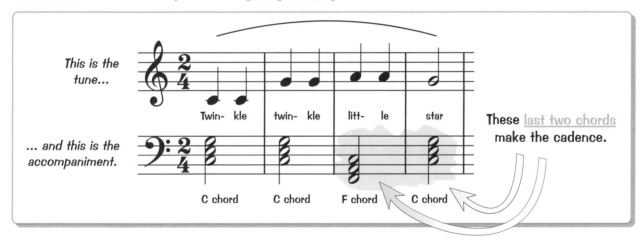

These last two chords make the cadence.

There are Four Main Types of Cadence

These pairs of chords are only cadences when they come at the end of a phrase. Anywhere else in a phrase, they're just chords.

Second Last Chord	Last Chord	Cadence
Chord V	Chord I	PERFECT
Chord IV	Chord I	PLAGAL
Chord I, II or IV	Chord V	IMPERFECT
Chord V	Any except Chord I (often Chord VI)	INTERRUPTED

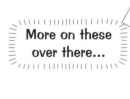
More on these over there...

Cadences

It's no good just knowing the <u>names</u> of the different cadences. You need to know what they're <u>used for</u>.

Perfect <u>and</u> Plagal Cadences <u>Work Like</u> Full Stops

1) A <u>PERFECT CADENCE</u> makes a piece of music feel <u>finished or complete</u>.

2) It goes from <u>Chord V</u> to <u>Chord I</u> — in C major that's a <u>G chord</u> to a <u>C chord</u>.

3) This is how a perfect cadence goes at the <u>end</u> of 'Twinkle, Twinkle, Little Star':

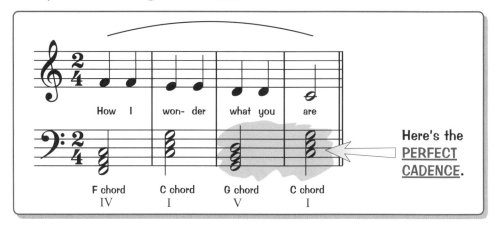

Here's the <u>PERFECT CADENCE</u>.

4) A <u>PLAGAL CADENCE</u> sounds really different from a perfect cadence but it has a <u>similar effect</u> — it makes a piece of music sound finished.

5) A plagal cadence in C major is an <u>F chord</u> (IV) to a <u>C chord</u> (I). Play it and see what it sounds like. The plagal cadence gets used at the <u>end</u> of lots of <u>hymns</u> — it's sometimes called the '<u>Amen</u>' cadence.

Imperfect <u>and</u> Interrupted Cadences <u>are Like</u> Commas

1) <u>Imperfect</u> and <u>interrupted</u> cadences are used to end <u>phrases</u> but <u>not</u> at the end of a piece. They work like <u>commas</u> — they feel like a <u>resting point</u> but not an ending.

2) An <u>IMPERFECT CADENCE</u> most commonly goes from chord <u>I</u>, <u>II</u> or <u>IV</u> to <u>V</u>. Here's one going from <u>chord I</u> to <u>chord V</u> at the end of the <u>third line</u> of 'Twinkle, Twinkle':

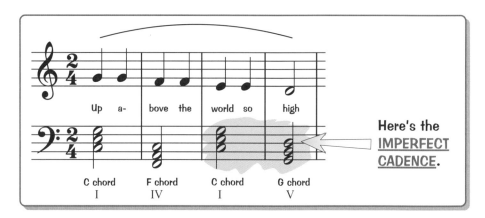

Here's the <u>IMPERFECT CADENCE</u>.

3) In an <u>INTERRUPTED CADENCE</u> chord V can go to any chord <u>except I</u>. You expect it to go to chord I — so it sounds "interrupted". In C major an interrupted cadence may go from a <u>G chord</u> (V) to an <u>Am chord</u> (VI).

The seventh plagal was the plagal of frogs...

This is another of those topics that isn't going to make much sense unless you sit down at a keyboard and <u>have a go</u>. Read it through again, and <u>play</u> the cadences until you can <u>hear</u> the differences between them. And then <u>learn it all</u> off by heart. Off by heart I said. Not half-hearted. Learn it <u>all</u>.

Modulation

Most of the notes in a piece of music come from one key — but to vary the tune or harmony you can modulate — change key. It can happen just once, or a few times in a piece. It's up to the composer.

The Starting Key is Called the Home Key

1) The key a piece starts out in is called the home key.
2) If the music's modulated it goes into a different key.
3) The change of key is only temporary.
4) However much a piece modulates, it usually ends in the home key.

There are Two Ways to Modulate

1) Modulation by Pivot Chord

1) A pivot chord is a chord that's in the home key and the key the music modulates to.
2) Chord V (G, B, D) in C major is exactly the same as chord I in G major — so it can be used to pivot between C major and G major.
3) Sometimes, the key signature changes to show the new key. More often, accidentals are written in the music where they're needed.

The home key here is C. At the end of the first bar the accompaniment uses the chord G, B, D to pivot into G major:

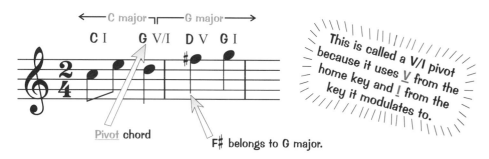

Pivot chord

F♯ belongs to G major.

This is called a V/I pivot because it uses V from the home key and I from the key it modulates to.

RELATED KEYS...

1) It sounds best if you modulate to related keys.
2) The closest keys are keys IV, V and the relative minor.
3) The next closest are the relative minors of keys IV and V.

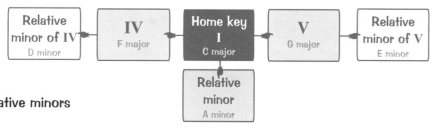

2) Abrupt Modulation

1) In abrupt modulation there's no pivot chord, and no other preparation either. It just happens.
2) Often the modulation is between two keys just one semitone apart, e.g. from C major to C♯ major.
3) Pop songs often modulate up one semitone. It creates a sudden, dramatic effect — it's meant to give the music an excited, uplifting feeling.

You can choose related keys but you can't choose your family...

If you see accidentals it often means the music's modulated, but not always.
The accidental could also be there because: 1) the music's written in a minor key — harmonic or melodic (see p.16), or 2) the composer fancied a spot of chromatic decoration (see p.28).

Texture

Here's one last way composers vary the harmony — by changing the texture. Texture's quite a bizarre word to use about music — what it means is how the chords and melody are woven together.

Monophonic Music is the Simplest

In monophonic music there's no harmony — just one line of tune. Monophonic music has a thin texture.

In contrast, harmonic music has harmony parts too — see below.

Polyphonic Music Weaves Tunes Together

1) Polyphonic music gives quite a complex effect because there's more than one tune being played at once.

2) It's sometimes called contrapuntal music.
3) Parts that move in contrary motion (one part goes up and another goes down) are polyphonic.

In Homophonic Music, the Parts Move Together

1) If the lines of music move at more or less the same time, it's homophonic music.
2) Melody and chords (chordal music) is a good example.
3) Parallel motion (when parts move with the same interval between them, e.g. parallel 5ths) is also homophonic.

In Heterophonic Music the Instruments Share the Tune

In heterophonic music there's one tune. All the instruments play it, but with variations, and often at different times.

Polyphonic, homophonic and heterophonic music all have quite a thick texture.

These are Other Ways of Varying Texture

SOLO one voice or instrument on its own

DUET 2-part piece

TRIO 3-part piece

QUARTET 4-part piece

UNISON all voices or instruments playing the same notes

TUTTI all instruments or voices playing at the same time

DOUBLING one part playing exactly the same notes as another

DESCANT part that runs along higher than the main melody

The Polyphonics — just East of Micronesia...

It's hard talking about texture — a bit like trying to describe a smell... If you need to write about texture in your listening test, these are handy words to use: smooth, dense, thick, heavy, light, thin... Go and get a thesaurus and scribble a few more words down, just in case.

Revision Summary

There's a lot to remember in this section: all four types of triad, all four types of inversion for triads, all those cadences, all the different ways of using decoration with chords, modulation, <u>and</u> what all those blah-phonic words mean. It's a right <u>old hairy mammoth</u> of a section and there's no way you'll get it all down in one mouthful. Chop the fearsome beast into tiny bite-size portions, and glue each one firmly to the cavern of your brain before you go attempt the next one. You'll know you've minced it fine enough when you can answer all these questions easily <u>without</u> looking back.

1) What's a chord?
2) Why can't you play a chord on a clarinet?
3) What do you call chords with:
   a) clashing notes   b) notes that sound good together?
4) How many notes are there in a triad?
5) The first note of a triad's called the root. What are the other two notes called?
6) What do you call a triad with B♭ as the root note?
7) How is a major third interval different from a minor third?
8) What are the two most common types of triad? Describe how you make each one.
9) What are the two less popular *(less loved, sniff)* triads called?
10) What makes a 7th chord different from a triad?
11) Write down the letter symbols for these chords:
    a) G major   b) A minor with a major 7th   c) D diminished chord   d) G augmented chord
12) Draw the scale of G major on a stave, then build a triad on each note. *(Don't forget the F sharps.)*
13) What's a harmonic progression?
14) Which three chords of any major or minor scale are known as the 'primary' triads?
15) Write out the notes of the three primary triads in C major, G major and D major.
16) Why don't composers use primary triads all the time?
17) Where do the root, third and fifth go in:
    a) a first inversion chord   b) a second inversion chord?
18) What kind of chords can have a third inversion?
19) Are these chords in root position, first inversion, second inversion or third inversion?
    a) 6/4   b) C/E   c) IVa   d) 6/4/2
20) How do you work out the root note of an inverted chord?
21) Name and describe four different chord figurations.
22) What's a drone?
23) What's melodic decoration?
24) What's the difference between a 'diatonic' decoration and a 'chromatic' decoration?
25) Explain the following terms:
    a) auxiliary note   b) passing note   c) an appoggiatura   d) a suspension
26) Write a one-sentence definition of a musical phrase.
27) What job does a cadence do in a phrase?
28) How many chords make up a cadence?
29) Write down the four different types of cadence and which chords you can use to make each one.
30) What's the difference between perfect and plagal cadences, and interrupted and imperfect cadences?
31) What's modulation? Name and describe the two different types.
32) Draw a diagram with G major at the centre, showing the most closely related keys.
33) What do people mean when they talk about the 'texture' of music?
34) Explain the difference between monophonic, homophonic, polyphonic and heterophonic music.
35) What is contrary motion?
36) What is parallel motion?
37) What do you call three musicians playing together? *(this is not a joke)*
38) What's the Italian word used when all the parts are played at the same time?

How Music's Organised

Music isn't just random notes — it's carefully organised, or at least it's meant to be.
Planning and organising makes music sound better, and makes it easier to write.

Music Needs Form and Structure

1) Music's got to be organised, or it just sounds like lots of plinky-plonky notes.
2) The most basic bit of organisation is the beats of a bar. The next biggest chunk is the phrasing.
3) The overall shape is called the structure or form.
4) The structure could be, e.g. the verses and chorus in a pop song, or the movements of a symphony.
5) Composers usually plan the structure of a piece of music before they get into the detail.

Most Musical Plans Use Repetition Repetition Repetition ...

1) Repetition means using a musical idea — a chunk of tune — more than once.
2) Repeating bits is a really good way of giving music shape. Once the audience know a tune it works like a landmark — they know where they are when they hear that tune later in the piece. (That's how choruses work, of course.)
3) If you're planning your own piece of music try repeating the best part of the tune.

...and Contrast

See p.35 & p.36 for more on repetition and contrast.

1) Repetition is really important — but constant repetition is boring.
2) Good compositions balance repetition with contrast. The aim is to do something different from the repeated bits to add variety.
3) There's contrast in just about every piece of music.
4) The verse and chorus structure of a pop song (see p.38) is one of the most obvious ways of using contrast.

If You're Composing, Plan the Structure First

1) Making a musical plan helps to organise your ideas — it's a bit like writing an essay plan.
2) It's OK to design your own musical plan, but a lot of people use 'tried and tested' plans like the ones described in the rest of this section, because they know they'll work.
3) 'Tried and tested' plans are like templates. The general organisation of the music is decided for you — you just need to add the details.

Learn to Spot the Plan When You're Listening to Music

In your listening exam, you'll need to recognise and write about the basic structure of the music.
To help you work it out, ask yourself these questions as you're listening...

- Which bits are repeated?
- Is there a main idea that gets repeated more than once? How many times do you hear it?
- Are there any contrasting ideas? How many? What's different about them?
- Is there a special introduction or ending section?
- Does the music have a plan similar to a piece you already know?

Holst was very organised — he always plan it...

The thing nobody mentions about repetition is, it's a lot less effort to repeat a good tune than make up a new one. Bear it in mind if you're a bit lazy like me. The thing nobody mentions about repetition is, it's a lot less effort to repeat a good tune than make up a new one. Bear it in mind if you're a bit lazy like me.

Binary, Ternary & Rondo Form

The binary, ternary and rondo forms are pretty simple — but make sure you learn them.

Binary Form has Two Sections

1) Binary means in two parts — there are two bits to a piece of music in binary form.

2) To make it easier to talk about the two bits you usually call the first one A and the second one B.

3) Each section is repeated. You play A twice, and then B twice — so you end up with AABB.

4) Section B contrasts with section A — the two parts should sound different.

5) The contrast's often made by modulating (see p.31).

6) The first modulation comes at the end of Section A. At the end of Section B the piece modulates back to the original key.

7) If you start in a major key, modulate to the dominant key (V), e.g. C major to G major.

8) If you start in a minor key, modulate to the relative major, e.g. A minor to C major.

SECTION A — first idea   *SECTION B — second, contrasting idea*

This symbol means "repeat the section".

Ternary Form has Three Sections

1) Ternary means in three parts — there are three sections in music with ternary form.

2) Each section repeats, so it goes AABBAA.

SECTION A — first idea   *SECTION B — second, contrasting idea*   *SECTION A — first idea*

There's a step-by-step guide to writing a piece in ternary on p.44.

3) Section A ends in the main key, normally with a perfect cadence (see p.30). This makes it sound like a complete piece in itself.

4) In Section B the music modulates to a related key, like the dominant or relative major or minor, and then goes back to the main key before it ends.

5) When the music goes back to A for the last section it can be exactly the same or varied a bit, e.g. with ornaments (see p.13). If it is varied you call it A1 instead of A.

6) A1 can be different but not so different that you can't tell it's a variation of A.

Rondo Form can have Any Number of Sections

1) Rondo means going round. A rondo starts with a main idea in section A, moves into a new section, goes round again to A, moves into another new section, goes round again to A... as many times as you like. The new section after each Section A always contrasts with A.

2) Section A is known as the main theme. The contrasting sections are called episodes.

SECTION A — main theme   *SECTION B — contrasting episode*   *SECTION A — main theme*   *SECTION C — another contrasting episode*   *SECTION A — main theme*

3) The main theme is always in the main key (home key). Each episode tends to modulate to a related key to create contrast.

4) The most important thing to remember is that after every new section, Section A always comes back. It literally does keep 'going round'.

I'm confused — what's quandary form...

In the listening test, when you're all flushed and panicky, this trick of using letters as shorthand is very handy indeed. As you're listening, put A for the first bit, B for a new bit, A1 for a variation of A... and so on. It's quick and clear — you should end up with a plan of the music that's easy to recognise.

Variations

Variations are pieces which start with one pattern or tune, and then change it in different ways.
There are two main structures for variation, called theme and variation and ground bass.

Theme and Variation Form Varies the Melody

1) Theme is another name for the main musical idea of a piece.

2) In theme and variation form, the theme's usually a memorable tune.

3) The theme's played first, then there's a short pause before the first variation's played, then another pause before the next variation. Each variation is a self-contained piece of music. There can be as many or as few variations as the composer wants.

4) Each variation should be a recognisable version of the main theme, but different from all the others.

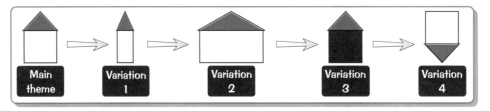

5) Many composers pick an existing tune — like Greensleeves or Twinkle, Twinkle — to use as the theme and then make up their own variations.

You can vary a theme by using any of these techniques.
Listen for them in the exam, and use them when you're composing.

1) Add notes to make the tune more complex — see ornamentation on p.13.

2) Remove notes to simplify the tune.

3) Change the length of the notes. It's called diminution or augmentation — see p.46.

4) a) Turn the melody upside down. This is called melodic inversion — see p.46.
   b) Turn the melody back-to-front. This is called retrograde, e.g. CDEG becomes GEDC.
   c) Turn the melody upside down and back-to-front. This is called retrograde inversion.

5) Add a countermelody — an extra melody over the top of the theme.

6) Change the key (tonality) — from major to minor.

7) Change the tempo — make the theme faster or slower.

8) Change the metre — say, from two beats in a bar to three.

9) Change some or all of the chords in the harmony — see Section 4.

10) Add a different accompaniment pattern to suggest a particular style, e.g. an 'oom pa pa' waltz pattern, an off-beat syncopated jazzy rhythm or a classical 'Alberti bass' pattern (p.27).

Ground Bass Form Varies Ideas Over a Fixed Bass Part

1) Ground bass is a continuous set of variations — there are no pauses.

2) The main theme — called the ground — is a bass line which repeats throughout the piece.

3) Varying melodies and harmonies which become gradually more complex are played over the ground.

4) There are two types of seventeenth century dance that are in ground bass form — the chaconne and passacaglia. They're quite slow and stately.

I'd like a variation on the theme of ice cream please...

Variations are a great starting point for composition. Try borrowing a tune, from your favourite song or something, then compose your own set of variations. Use the ideas from the box to help you think about how to vary the theme. Even better, start off by composing your own theme.

Basic Structures for Songs

People have been writing songs for thousands of years and they've come up with a fair old number of song structures. What's more, a song structure never caused any death or pollution, I don't think.

Call and Response Sounds like a Conversation

1) A call and response structure has two bits to it:

> Part 1, the CALL, asks a question.   Part 2, the RESPONSE, gives an answer.

2) To give the feeling of question and answer, the call ends on note 5 or chord V — an imperfect cadence. The response ends on note 1 or chord I — a perfect cadence. (See p.29-30 for more on cadences.)

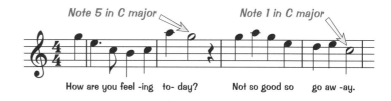

Note 5 in C major   Note 1 in C major

How are you feel -ing to- day?   Not so good so   go aw -ay.

3) Call and response works well in instrumental music as well as songs.

Songs can be Built on Riffs

1) A riff is a short repeated tune. If you put a few riffs together you can make a whole song.

2) A lot of rock music is riff-based. The bass guitar plays and repeats one short riff pattern. The rhythm guitar adds another harmonic riff and the drums add a rhythmic riff. The lead guitar adds a lead riff and the singer sings over all this. This creates one section of melody.

3) The riffs often change for the chorus.

Ballads Tell Stories

1) The word ballad was originally used in the 15th century. Back then it meant a long song with lots of verses that told a story. It's the type of thing that was sung by wandering minstrels.

2) If you hear people talking about ballads today they usually mean pop or rock ballads — songs that tell stories, often with a romantic or spooky twist that keeps people listening to the end.

3) Each verse has the same rhythm and tune.

12-Bar Blues Repeats a 12-Bar Structure

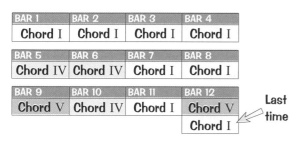

BAR 1	BAR 2	BAR 3	BAR 4
Chord I	Chord I	Chord I	Chord I

BAR 5	BAR 6	BAR 7	BAR 8
Chord IV	Chord IV	Chord I	Chord I

BAR 9	BAR 10	BAR 11	BAR 12
Chord V	Chord IV	Chord I	Chord V
			Chord I

Last time

1) In 12-bar blues the main structure is 12 bars long. (No kidding...)
2) The only chords are I, IV and V.
3) They're used in a set pattern through the 12 bars.
4) The 12-bar structure gets repeated through the song. To lead back into bar 1 you play chord V in bar 12 instead of chord I. Chord I is only actually played in bar 12 at the very end.
5) In the tune notes 3 and 7 are flattened — e.g. in G major, you play B♭ and F♮. These are the 'blue' notes (see p.18).

32-Bar Song Form is Very Very Simple

1) 32-bar song form breaks down into four 8-bar sections.
2) Sections 1, 2 and 4 use the main theme. Section 3 uses a contrasting theme.

Sing a song of sixpence — but I'd rather have twenty quid...

All these types of songs are just basic forms — there are millions of things you can do with each one to get different sounding songs. How else would record companies saturate the charts with dross...

Basic Structures for Songs

This humdinger of a page goes through the different bits of a pop song.
By which I mean any song of the kind you'd hear on Radio 1, not Radio 3.

The Main Sections are the Verse and Chorus

1) The verse always has the same tune, but the lyrics change in each verse.
2) The chorus has a different tune from the verse, usually quite a catchy one.
   The lyrics and tune of the chorus don't change.
3) The verse tells the story of the song. The chorus backs up the message of the story.
4) In a lot of songs, the verse and the chorus are both 8 bars long. This gives the song a balanced feel.
5) Most songs go verse, chorus, verse, chorus, etc. But there's no rule about this. You can use verses and choruses in any order you like, e.g. chorus, verse, verse, chorus, verse, chorus. It's up to you.

The Middle 8 is an Example of a Bridge

1) The middle 8 is an 8-bar section that's put into the middle of the song.
   It has new chords, new lyrics and a whole new feel.
2) The idea is to stop the listeners from getting bored with the repeated
   verse and chorus. Just about every pop song has a middle 8.
3) A more general term for a 'break' in the song is a bridge. A bridge doesn't have to be 8 bars long.
   Bridges are used to link different sections — verse and chorus, verse and verse, a slow bit and a fast bit...

A Song Needs an Intro and a Coda

Intro

Coda

INTRODUCTION

1) Introductions have two jobs. They grab the audience's attention and set the mood for the song.
2) If you're writing an intro it's a good idea to do it last, so you can use the best bit from the song to make people sit up and listen.

CODA

1) The coda (or 'outro') is an ending that's different from the verse and the chorus.
2) You can use the coda to create a big finish, or just fade out.

Instrumentals Let the Players Show Off

1) An instrumental section is one of those bits where the singer has a rest, and somebody else — maybe the lead guitar or keyboard — gets to play their little hearts out.
2) They're no trouble to write (or improvise) because they use the same chords as the verse or chorus.
3) It sounds good to the listeners because they already know the chords, so the instrumental sounds familiar even on the first hearing.

Put all the bits together and you end up with something like this (though most songs won't have all these bits):

| INTRO | CHORUS | VERSE | CHORUS | VERSE | MIDDLE 8 | CHORUS | BRIDGE | INSTRU-MENTAL | CHORUS | CODA (OUTRO) |

All together now...

When you break songs up into bits like this and give them formal names and everything it makes it all sound really boring. Like maths or something. Rise above the boredom and learn the names — if you get this type of song in your listening test you'll get loads more marks for using the proper terms.

Sonata Form

Sonata form is a bit <u>tricky</u>, and given the choice I'd have left it out. But I'm afraid my hands are tied — if you want a top grade, you have to know this stuff. So strap yourself in and prepare for take-off...

A Piece in Sonata Form has Three Main Sections

| Exposition | → | Development | → | Recapitulation |

Themes are "exposed" — heard for the first time.

Themes go through a number of interesting twists and turns.

Themes are "recapped" — played again.

The Exposition has Two Themes

1) Having <u>two themes</u> lets you build up a <u>contrast</u> as you switch between them.

2) One theme could be <u>major</u> and the other <u>minor</u>. One could be <u>delicate</u> and the other <u>heavy</u>, or one could be <u>high</u> and the other <u>low</u>. It doesn't matter what the contrast is, so long as there *is* a contrast.

3) Some <u>Classical</u> sonatas have a slow-ish <u>introduction</u> before the main themes.

4) The exposition ends in a <u>different key</u> from the home key, and the whole section is marked to be <u>repeated</u>.

The Development Keeps the Piece Interesting

In the middle section the themes get taken through lots of <u>variations</u>. You can vary them any way you like:

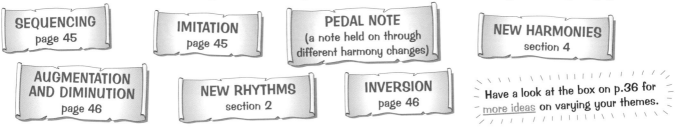

SEQUENCING
page 45

IMITATION
page 45

PEDAL NOTE
(a note held on through different harmony changes)

NEW HARMONIES
section 4

AUGMENTATION AND DIMINUTION
page 46

NEW RHYTHMS
section 2

INVERSION
page 46

Have a look at the box on p.36 for <u>more ideas</u> on varying your themes.

Classical composers often <u>mixed</u> these techniques, e.g. sequencing an augmented version of one of the themes. Mixing and matching like this gives you loads of <u>possibilities</u> for your variations.

The Recapitulation Pulls it All Together Again

1) If you're composing, this is the easy bit — the themes from the exposition are played <u>again</u>.

2) It's best not to do an <u>exact</u> repeat of the exposition. Make a few changes like adding <u>ornaments</u> (see p.13) or making the themes a bit <u>shorter</u>. This holds the listener's attention to the very <u>end</u>.

3) <u>Bridge sections</u> (see p.38) are used to link and modulate between two themes.

4) Composers usually add a coda (see p.38) to finish the piece off neatly. The traditional ending is a perfect cadence — but if it's your sonata, end it however you like.

5) For real <u>polish</u> add short link passages made up of <u>new material</u> between each of the three main sections. The final structure should look something like this:

| INTRODUCTION | EXPOSITION | DEVELOPMENT | RECAPITULATION | CODA |

BRIDGE (between themes) · LINK · LINK · BRIDGE (between themes)

It's complicated — but that's no excuse for not learning it...

Sonata form is <u>frightfully sophisticated</u>, dah-ling. Get on top of it and you can feel really smug. Don't get muddled up between <u>sonata form</u> and <u>sonatas</u>. Sonatas <u>use</u> sonata form in the first movement, and sometimes the last one too — have a look at <u>page 40</u> to find out more.

Sonatas, Symphonies & Concertos

The examiners won't expect you to write anything this massive, but you definitely need to know all about them for the listening test. And for polite dinner party conversation when you're about 40. Maybe.

Sonatas are for One or Two Instruments

1) Sonatas are mostly written for one instrument, but there are some sonatas for two instruments and a few for two types of instrument, each type playing a different part.

2) A sonata is usually in three or four sections (called movements), with breaks between them.

3) At least one of the movements is in sonata form (see p.39) — usually the first and sometimes the last.

A Symphony is Played by a Full Orchestra

1) A symphony is a massive piece. They can last more than an hour and have real impact because of the full orchestra.

2) A symphony has the same structure as a sonata. They more often have four movements rather than three (and can have more than four).

3) Some symphonies have a choir as well as the orchestra.

> These chaps were all keen symphony writers...

Haydn	Mozart	Beethoven	Schubert	Berlioz	Mendelssohn	Schumann	Brahms	Tchaikovsky	Mahler
1732 - 1809	1756 - 1791	1770 - 1827	1797 - 1828	1803 - 1869	1809 - 1847	1810 - 1856	1833 - 1897	1840 - 1893	1860 - 1911

A Concerto is for a Solo Instrument and an Orchestra

1) The soloist has most of the tune, and gets to really show off how brilliant they are.

2) The orchestra has the tune some of the time too though. Their part's a bit more than an accompaniment.

3) There are usually three movements — quick, slow and quick.

There are Standard Forms for 4-Movement Compositions

Sonatas, symphonies and concertos all follow the same basic plan. These are the traditional forms used by composers for each of the movements.

> This one's left out of sonatas in three movements and concertos.

FIRST MOVEMENT	sonata form	brisk and purposeful
SECOND MOVEMENT	ternary or variation form	slower and songlike
THIRD MOVEMENT	minuet or scherzo	fairly fast and dance-like
FOURTH MOVEMENT	rondo, variation or sonata form	fast and cheerful

Just one concerto, play it for me...

There are thousands of sonatas, symphonies and concertos. Western composers have been churning them out since the sixteenth century. In some ways they're quite similar, so learn this page really carefully, and make sure you know the differences — who plays them and how many movements they have.

Opera & Oratorio

Opera and oratorio are forms you'll need to know for listening. If you write a whole oratorio for your composition, the examiners will be so impressed they'll probably fall down in a faint. Very undignified.

Operas are like Plays set to Music

1) The main characters are played by solo singers.
2) The main characters are supported by a chorus and an orchestra.
3) The story is acted out — usually with lavish sets, costumes and special effects.
4) In some operas every single word is sung — in others there's a bit of talking from time to time.
5) Some operas have really serious, tragic themes. Others are more light-hearted and comic. These are the names for the main types.
6) The words of an opera are called the 'libretto'. This is often written by a 'librettist' working alongside the composer.

Grand opera	serious, set entirely to music
Opéra comique	some spoken dialogue
Opera buffa	comic opera
Opera seria	formal, serious opera

In Opera there are Three Types of Singing

ARIA
1) An aria is a solo vocal piece, backed by the orchestra.
2) Arias are used to go into the emotions of the main characters.
3) The arias have the memorable, exciting tunes. They're challenging for the performers and let them show their vocal tone and agility.

RECITATIVE
1) Recitative is a half-spoken, half-singing style used for some conversations.
2) Recitativo secco is recitative that's unaccompanied or backed by simple chords.
3) Recitativo stromentato or accompagnato is recitative with orchestral backing. The accompaniment's used to increase the dramatic tension of the words.

CHORUS — A bit where the whole chorus sings together.

Oratorio is the Religious Version of Opera

1) An oratorio has arias, recitatives and choruses just like an opera.
2) Oratorios usually have a religious theme. They're based on traditional stories, sometimes from the Bible.
3) Oratorios don't usually have scenery, costumes or action — they're not acted out.
4) Oratorios were written mainly for concert or church performance.

Composer	Lived	Famous Oratorio
Carissimi	1605 - 1674	Jephte
Handel	1685 - 1759	Messiah
Haydn	1732 - 1809	The Creation
Berlioz	1803 - 1869	L'Enfance du Christ
Mendelssohn	1809 - 1847	Elijah
Elgar	1857 - 1934	The Dream of Gerontius
Walton	1902 - 1983	Belshazzar's Feast

The show ain't over till the fat lady sings...

Actually, nowadays, most opera singers are pretty skinny. The women are, anyway. In olden times (up until about twenty years ago) they used to think they'd lose their singing powers if they lost weight. They also used to swallow live worms to make their voices smooth and lovely. Or so I've been told.

Smaller Vocal Pieces

These songs are shorter than operas and the like, but you still need to know their forms...

Lots of Music was Written to be Sung in Church

CANTATA

Some things in a cantata are similar to oratorio. The performers are solo singers, a chorus and an orchestra. There's no scenery and no acting and they were written to be performed in a church or concert hall.

The difference is that the words are taken from books or poems — they're not specially written. Most cantatas have a religious theme — but not all of them.

CHORALE

Chorales are hymns. They have simple language and a melody that's easy to sing. J.S. Bach wrote stacks of them. Here's a bit from a chorale he put in *St. Matthew's Passion*.

O Lord, who dares to smite Thee?

MOTET & ANTHEM

A motet's a short piece written to be performed by the choir in church. They're written for Roman Catholic churches and the words are often in Latin. Motets are polyphonic — see p.32.

An anthem is very similar to a motet except they're written for Protestant churches, so the words aren't in Latin.

MASS

The mass is the name of a Roman Catholic church service — these parts of the mass are sung by the choir, or the choir and soloists:

Musical settings of the Mass were originally written to be used in church, but nowadays they're played in concerts, too. The text is usually in Latin.

- Kyrie — *Lord have mercy...*
- Gloria — *Glory be to God on high...*
- Credo — *I believe in one God...*
- Sanctus — *Holy, holy, holy...*
- Benedictus — *Blessed is He...*
- Agnus Dei — *O Lamb of God...*

(Some of them are quite long, so I've only given you the starting bits.)

Madrigals and Lieder are non-Religious

Most madrigals were written in the 1500s and 1600s. They're about love or the countryside — or both. Most have no accompaniment and each person sings a different part. Madrigals often use imitation (see p.45).

Now is the month of May -ing, When mer-ry lads are play-ing: Fa la la la la la la la la la, Fa la la la la la la.

A lied's a song for one singer and a piano. Both parts are equally important. The words really matter too — they're usually based on poems. Lieder were massively popular in the German Romantic period (late 18th to early 19th century).

To wan -der is the mil -ler's joy, to wan -der

From *The Wandering Miller* by Schubert. He wrote over 600 top quality lieder.

They don't seem to have mentioned karaoke...

'Lied' is the German word for 'song'. It's pronounced LEED. If you're talking about more than one lied you say lieder (not 'lieds'). Here endeth the German lesson.

Revision Summary

This section's been a living nightmare of technical terms, tricky ideas and generally complex stuff that needs remembering. But lookee here... what light through yonder cloud of revision gloom breaks? It is the revision summary questions, and they will save your skin. When you feel like you've got to grips with the section, have a go at these. When you can answer them all <u>without</u> looking back, you really <u>have</u> got to grips with the section...

1) Give an example of a structure you could use when composing.

2) How many sections are there in a piece in:
   a) binary form   b) ternary form?

3) Is a piece that's organised "A, B, A1" in binary form, or ternary form?

4) What does *rondo* mean?

5) How many sections are there in a piece in rondo form?

6) When you use letters to stand for the names of the different sections, does "B" stand for:
   a) main theme   b) a contrasting episode?

7) Is theme and variation form one continuous piece of music, or are there gaps between sections?

8) Write down six different ways you can vary the main theme in a theme and variation piece.

9) What are the main differences between theme and variation form and ground bass form?

10) In call and response, what type of cadences end the "call" and the "response"?

11) What's a riff?

12) What do the lyrics do in a ballad?

13) What chords do you get in 12-bar blues?

14) How do you make a 12-bar blues song longer than 12 bars?

15) Draw a diagram of a song in 32-bar song form, using a labelled box for each section.

16) Write true or false for each of these. In a pop song:
   a) the verse has the same words every time
   b) the chorus tells the story
   c) the middle 8 sounds much the same as the verse and chorus
   d) when James Brown said "Take it to the bridge" he meant the Hammersmith Flyover
   e) the intro is always quiet

17) What order do these sections come in, in sonata form? Development, Exposition, Recapitulation.

18) Write down at least five ways of varying the themes in a sonata.

19) Where would you use an introduction, coda, links and bridges in sonata form?

20) Write down how many performers there are, how many movements there are and what the movements are like for each of these: a) sonata   b) symphony   c) concerto.

21) What are the words of an opera called?

22) What are the three main singing styles in an opera?

23) Write down one difference and one similarity between opera and oratorio.

24) What's the difference between a motet and an anthem?

25) Write down the six main parts of a mass.

26) When were madrigals written?

27) How many performers perform a lied?

Coming Up with a Composition

Using all the bits and bobs from the last five sections, you should be able to write a piece of your own now. If you're not sure where to start, try following these instructions for a composition in ternary form.

1) Start by Working Out an 8-Bar Rhythm

1) First compose a 4-bar rhythm. End it in a longish note, e.g. crotchet or minim. This is the question phrase.

2) Compose another 4-bar rhythm. This is the answering phrase. End on a long note and repeat some of the rhythm patterns from the question in the answer.

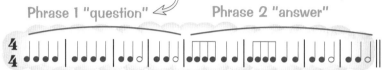

Phrase 1 "question"   Phrase 2 "answer"

3) Don't worry about the pitch of the notes, just sort out the rhythm.

2) Turn the Rhythm into a Melody

1) Choose a scale to get your notes from. C major's dead easy — it only uses the white notes on the keyboard — C, D, E, F, G, A, B and C.

2) Make the first and last note of your melody the same as note 1 of your scale. In C major it's C.

3) Make the last note of bar 4 the same as note 5 of your scale. Note 5 of C major is G.

It's fine to use the same note several times.

4) Give the rest of the notes letter names from your scale. The melody will sound better if it moves up and down in steps or with just small leaps.

3) Write Another 8 Bars to get a Piece in Ternary Form

1) A piece in ternary form (p.35) has three sections, two the same, and one different — ABA.

2) You've already got Section A — it's your 8-bar composition. For Section B compose another 8 bars the same way you did for Section A.

3) Section B needs to contrast with Section A. An easy-ish way is to use a different scale, related to the one you used for Section A (see p.17 and p.31). E.g. if Section A's in C major you could put Section B in the dominant key — G major, or the relative minor — A minor.

4) Play ABA and you've got a complete piece in ternary form.

4) Add a Harmony

1) If you want to add a harmony have a look at Section 4 on chords.

2) It works well to include the note you're harmonising with in the chord.

3) Always use cadences (p.29-30) to finish off phrases.

Compose yourself — this isn't that bad...

Checking's never a bad idea. Check that the beats in every bar add up to the number of beats in the time signature. Check that you haven't got any notes from random keys. The best thing to do is play it.

<u>*Ways to Vary a Composition*</u>

There are lots of ways composers make their <u>rhythms</u> and <u>melodies</u> more interesting. Even if you don't want to use these yourself, learn what they're called, in case they come up in your listening test.

<u>Sandwich Contrasting Melodies</u>

1) If a simple <u>phrase</u> works well you can <u>repeat it</u>.

2) For variety, put a <u>contrasting</u> phrase between the repeated bits.

<u>Repeat a Pattern, Vary the Pitch</u>

1) Repeat the <u>pattern</u> of a phrase but start on a <u>different note</u>, higher or lower. This is called a <u>sequence</u>.

2) You can repeat the phrase in a sequence <u>as many times as you like</u>. This is called <u>sequencing</u>.

<u>Keep Repeating the Phrase with Slight Changes — Imitation</u>

1) In <u>imitation</u> a phrase is repeated with <u>slight changes</u> each time — each phrase <u>imitates</u> the one before.

2) It works particularly well if one instrument or voice imitates <u>another</u> and then <u>overlaps</u>.

3) Imitation was especially popular with composers in the <u>Baroque period</u>.

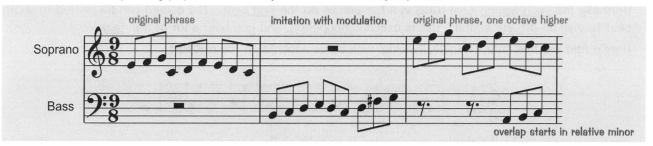

<u>Keep One Pattern the Same, Change the Rest — Ostinato</u>

1) One pattern's played <u>over and over again</u>.

2) The <u>rest of the piece</u> changes round it.

3) This is called an <u>ostinato</u>. It's found in all sorts of music, from medieval to pop to African. This is sort of boogie-woogie...

> <u>Riffs</u> (see p.37) are basically ostinatos going by a less fancy name.

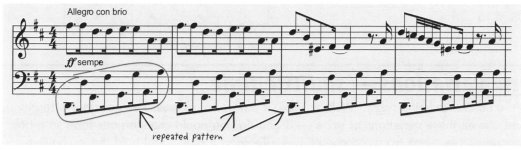

repeated pattern

Ways to Vary a Composition

Change the _Rhythm_

You can get a new version of the melody by <u>lengthening</u> or <u>shortening</u> the notes.

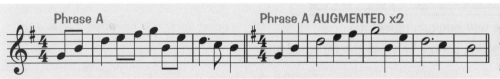

Making all the notes longer is called <u>augmentation</u>. The length of each note's <u>multiplied</u> by the same amount.

Making all the notes shorter by the same amount is called <u>diminution</u>.

Remember — this is to do with <u>time</u>. <u>DON'T</u> get it mixed up with augmented and diminished <u>intervals</u> — they're all about <u>pitch</u>.

Turn the Tune _Upside down_

1) You can turn a phrase or a melody <u>upside down</u> — this is known as <u>melodic inversion</u>.
2) You keep the <u>same intervals</u> between the notes, but they go in the <u>opposite direction</u>, i.e. down instead of up and up instead of down.

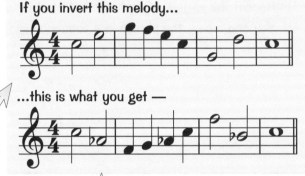

If you invert this melody...

...this is what you get —

The first melody goes <u>up a third</u> from C to E, then up another third to G.

In the inversion the melody goes <u>down a third</u> to A♭, then down another third from A♭ to F.

Jazz Up _the_ Rhythms

1) Normally the <u>main accent</u> (see p.12) in a bar comes on the <u>first beat</u>. The accent can be shifted to another beat to give an <u>offbeat</u> sound. This is called <u>syncopation</u>, and you hear a lot of it in <u>jazz</u>.

Here's that old favourite, 'Twinkle, Twinkle' with some accents on the offbeat:

2) Another way to make the rhythm syncopated is to shift <u>all</u> the accents across by the <u>same</u> amount, like so:

3) If the beats are divided up in <u>different ways</u> and the accents fall in <u>different places</u> in the different parts, it's called <u>cross-rhythm</u>.

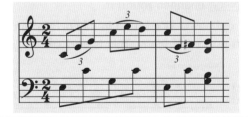

So many variations — so little time...

Composing's a bit like ordering <u>pizza</u>. Well, actually it's not, but at least I've got your attention. Don't try and use all these variations at once — if you do you could change your tune so much that it's unrecognisable. Just try using one or two effects at a time. And hold the <u>anchovies</u>.

Revision Summary

Well, that was short — some might say sweet. I'll just say it was short. If you want to have a go at writing a ternary form piece the way I described on p.44 then you are GREAT. But unfortunately I can't test you on it because I can't hear it. I mean, you could send me a tape, but maybe I would have moved house when it arrived, or maybe it would get lost in the post. Anyway, the point is the questions here are all about the different ways of making compositions more <u>varied</u>, and a good thing too because this is stuff that could save your skin for composing <u>and</u> listening. Read on and answer away.

1) If you're repeating a melody because it's so amazingly good, what should you put between the repeated phrases to keep the audience listening?

2) You've got a lovely phrase and you decide to reuse it. You repeat it at a higher pitch. You repeat it at a lower pitch. You repeat it at the original pitch. You repeat it at an even lower pitch. What's the proper name for this technique?

3) Suggest two ways you could change a phrase using imitation.

4) In which period was imitation used a lot?

5) What is ostinato?

6) Write out a tune you know on a treble clef stave, then write a diminished version and an augmented version.

7) Describe what is meant by an inversion.

8) Write a definition for each of these ways of varying the beat:
   a) offbeat
   b) syncopated
   c) cross-rhythm

Brass Instruments

You probably know quite a bit about your instrument. But it helps when you're playing or singing with other people to know a bit about their instruments too, so you can understand what they're up to. Brass first.

Brass Instruments are All Made of Metal (though not always brass...)

1) Brass instruments are horns, trumpets, cornets, trombones and tubas.

2) They're all basically a length of hollow, metal tubing with a mouthpiece (the bit you blow into) at one end and a funnel shape (the bell) at the other.

3) The different shapes and sizes of these parts gives each brass instrument a different tone and character.

You Get a Noise by 'Buzzing' your Lips

1) To make a sound on a brass instrument, you have to make the air vibrate down the tube.

2) You do it by 'buzzing' your lips into the mouthpiece. You squeeze your lips together, then blow through a tiny gap so you get a buzzing noise. You know you've got it right when it really tickles.

3) You have to squeeze your lips together tighter to get higher notes.

4) Notes can be slurred (played together smoothly) or tongued (you use your tongue to separate the notes).

Brass Instruments Use Slides and Valves to Change Pitch

1) Squeezing your lips only gets a limited range of notes. To get a decent range brass instruments use slides (like on a trombone) or valves (like on a trumpet).

2) The slide on a trombone is the U-shaped tube that moves in and out of the main tube. Moving it out makes the tube longer so you get a lower note. Moving it in makes the tube shorter so you get a higher note.

3) Horns, trumpets and cornets use three buttons connected to valves. The valves open and close different sections of the tube to make it longer or shorter. Pressing down the buttons in different combinations gives you all the notes you need.

Brass Players use Mutes to Change the Tone

1) A mute is a kind of bung that's put in the bell of a brass instrument. It's used to make the instrument play more quietly and change the tone. You wouldn't usually use one all the way through a piece — just for a short section.

2) Different shapes and sizes of mute change the tone in different ways, e.g. the wowwow mute gives the instrument a wowwow sound. I bet you never would have guessed...

Brassed off — how could you be, revising's so much fun...

If you get brass in a listening test and need to say what instrument it is, remember the bigger instruments generally play lower notes and smaller instruments play higher notes. Brass instruments are by far the best instruments to play — ask any brass player. I'm a brass player, but I'm not biased at all.

Woodwind

People sometimes get woodwind and brass muddled up. If you're one of them <u>learn the difference</u>.

Woodwind Instruments used to be Made of Wood

<u>Woodwind</u> instruments got their name because they all use <u>air</u> — wind — to make a sound and once upon a time, they were all made of <u>wood</u>. Nowadays some are still made of wood, but others are made of <u>plastic</u> or <u>silver</u>. These are the main ones:

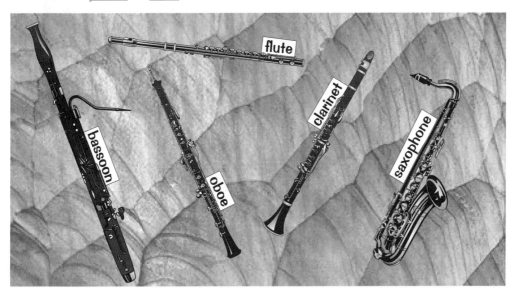

Woodwind Instruments Make Sound in Different Ways

To get a <u>sound</u> from a <u>wind</u> instrument, you have to make the <u>air</u> in its tube <u>vibrate</u>. There are <u>three different ways</u> woodwind instruments do this:

1) <u>EDGE-TONE INSTRUMENTS</u> — <u>flutes</u> and <u>piccolos</u>. Air's blown across an <u>oval-shaped hole</u>. The <u>edge</u> of the hole <u>splits</u> the air. This makes it <u>vibrate</u> down the instrument and make the sound.

2) <u>SINGLE-REED INSTRUMENTS</u> — <u>clarinets</u> and <u>saxophones</u>. Air is blown down a mouthpiece which has a <u>reed</u> — a thin slice of wood/reed/plastic — clamped to it. The reed <u>vibrates</u>, making the air in the instrument <u>vibrate</u>, and creating the sound.

3) <u>DOUBLE-REED INSTRUMENTS</u> — <u>oboes</u> and <u>bassoons</u>. The air passes between <u>two reeds</u>, tightly bound together and squeezed between the lips. The reeds <u>vibrate</u> and you get a sound.

Like brass instruments, woodwind instruments can be <u>slurred</u> or <u>tongued</u> as well.

Different Notes are made by Opening and Closing Holes

1) Wind instruments are covered in <u>keys</u>, <u>springs</u> and <u>levers</u>. These operate little <u>pads</u> that <u>close</u> and <u>open</u> holes down the instrument.

2) Opening and closing holes effectively makes the instrument longer or shorter. The <u>shorter</u> the tube, the <u>higher</u> the note. The <u>longer</u> the tube, the <u>lower</u> the note.

I can't see the woodwind for the clarinets...

Flutes and saxophones are made of metal but they're still <u>wood</u>wind instruments. If you're still confused remember that woodwind instruments sound more <u>breathy</u>, and brass instruments sound, well... farty...

Orchestral Strings

Orchestral strings are the <u>heart</u> of the orchestra — or so string players would have you believe.

The <u>Double Bass, Cello, Viola</u> and <u>Violin</u> are Very Alike

These are all <u>made</u> and played in a <u>similar way</u>.
The main differences are the <u>size</u> and <u>pitch</u>.

Stringed Instruments can be <u>Bowed</u> or <u>Plucked</u>

bow (made of wood and hair). The hair is drawn across the strings.

When the <u>strings vibrate</u>, the air inside the instrument <u>vibrates</u> and makes a <u>sound</u>.
There are two ways to get the strings vibrating:

1) <u>Bowing</u> — drawing a bow across the string. *Con arco* (or just *arco*) means '<u>with bow</u>'.

2) <u>Plucking</u> the string with the tip of your finger. The posh word for this is *pizzicato*.

The Strings are 'Stopped' to Make Different Notes

1) You can get an <u>open note</u> just by plucking or bowing one of the four strings.

2) To get all the other notes, you have to change the <u>length</u> of the strings.
You do this by <u>pressing down</u> with your finger. It's called <u>stopping</u>.

3) If you stop a string <u>close to the bridge</u>, the string's short and you get a <u>high</u> note.

4) If you stop a string <u>further away</u> from the bridge, the string's longer and you get a <u>lower</u> note.

5) <u>Double-stopping</u> is when <u>two</u> notes are played at the same time. Both strings are <u>pressed</u> (not open).

You Can Get Very Varied Effects with String Instruments

1) *TREMOLO* The bow's moved <u>back and forth</u> really <u>quickly</u>. This makes the notes sort of trembly. It's a great effect for making music sound <u>spooky</u> and <u>dramatic</u>.

2) *COL LEGNO* The <u>wood</u> of the bow is dragged across the strings instead of the <u>hair</u>.
This makes an <u>eerie</u>, <u>scraping</u> sound.

3) *CON SORDINO* A <u>mute</u> is put over the <u>bridge</u> (the piece of wood that supports the strings). It makes the sound <u>distant</u> and <u>soft</u>. Mutes are made of <u>wood</u> or <u>rubber</u>.

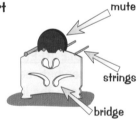
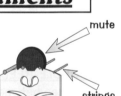

mute

strings

bridge

The Harp is Different...

1) The harp's <u>always plucked</u> — not bowed.

2) Most have <u>47</u> strings. Plucking each string in order is like playing up the <u>white notes</u> on a piano.

3) It has <u>seven pedals</u>. Pressing and releasing these lets you play <u>sharp</u> and <u>flat</u> notes.

4) You can play <u>one</u> note at a time, or play <u>chords</u> by plucking a few strings together.

Violinists are always in tears — too highly strung...

Violins are played in folk music, country, jazz and naff pop songs, and a jazz band would only be half there if it didn't have a double bass. So these instruments are often "<u>orchestral</u>" but <u>not always</u>.

Guitars

Guitars are bloomin' everywhere. So it's best to know a bit about how they work.

An Acoustic Guitar has a Hollow Body

The acoustic guitar makes a sound the same way as the orchestral strings — by vibrating air in its body. Slightly different types are used by pop, folk and classical guitarists, but the basic design is similar.

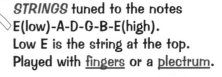

You can lose your plectrum in here.

HOLLOW BODY makes the string vibrations resonate, giving a louder sound.

STRINGS tuned to the notes E(low)-A-D-G-B-E(high). Low E is the string at the top. Played with fingers or a plectrum.

FRETS (the little metal strips on the fingerboard) help the player find the correct finger position for different notes.

acoustic guitar

There are three different kinds of acoustic guitar:

1) The classical or Spanish guitar — has nylon strings (the thickest three are covered in fine wire) and a thick neck.

2) The acoustic guitar — has steel strings and is used mainly in pop and folk music. Its neck is thinner and is strengthened with a metal bar — this supports the higher tension created by the steel strings.

3) The 12-stringed guitar — often used in folk music. There are two of each string — this gives a 'thicker' sound which works well for accompanying singing.

Electric Guitars Use an Amplifier and a Loudspeaker

1) An electric guitar has six strings, just like an acoustic guitar, and is played in a similar way.

2) The main difference is that an electric guitar has a solid body. The sound's made louder electrically, using an amplifier and a loudspeaker.

3) A combo — short for combination — is an amplifier and loudspeaker 'all in one'.

electric guitar

You can't lose your plectrum in here.

A semi-acoustic electric guitar has a hollow body to naturally amplify sounds and all the right fiddly knobs to be plugged in and played electrically.

The Bass Guitar Usually has Four Strings

1) The bass guitar works just the same way as the guitar, except it usually has four strings (though you can get bass guitars with five or six strings).

2) They're tuned to the notes E-A-D-G (from lowest note to highest).

3) It's lower pitched than other guitars because it has thicker and longer strings.

4) Most bass guitars have frets, but there are some — imaginatively named fretless basses — that don't.

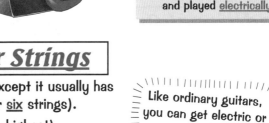

Like ordinary guitars, you can get electric or acoustic basses.

Guitar Strings are Picked or Strummed

1) Plucking one string at a time is called picking. Classical and lead guitarists pick the notes of a melody. Bass guitarists almost always pick out the individual notes of a bass line. They hardly ever strum.

2) Playing two or more strings at a time is called strumming. It's how you play chords. Pop and folk guitarists tend to play accompaniments rather than tunes, so they do more strumming than picking.

3) A plectrum is a small, flat piece of plastic that guitarists can use to pluck or strum with — it's kind of like having an extra long fingernail.

Who says the air guitar's not a proper instrument...

Learn those different playing techniques and if you hear them in the exam, use the proper words — picking and strumming — to describe them. The examiners'll think all their Christmases have come at once.

Keyboard Instruments

The actual <u>keyboard</u> looks much the same on most keyboard instruments, but the wires and mysterious levers <u>inside</u> vary quite a bit, and that means the <u>sounds</u> they make vary too.

Harpsichords, Virginals and Clavichords Came First

This fella's a harpsichord.

1) Harpsichords were invented long before pianos. They're still played today but they were <u>most popular</u> in the <u>Baroque</u> and <u>early Classical</u> periods.

2) Harpsichords have quite a <u>tinny</u>, <u>string</u> sound. When you press a key a string inside is <u>plucked</u> by a lever. You <u>can't vary</u> the <u>strength</u> of the pluck, so you <u>can't vary</u> the <u>dynamics</u>.

3) A <u>virginal</u> is a miniature table-top version of a harpsichord. Virginals were really popular in England in the <u>sixteenth century</u>.

4) The <u>clavichord</u> is another early keyboard instrument. Clavichords are small and have a <u>soft</u> sound. The strings are <u>struck</u> with hammers, not plucked, so you can vary the dynamics a little bit.

The Most Popular Keyboard Instrument Now is the Piano

1) The piano was invented around <u>1700</u>. The <u>technology</u> is <u>more sophisticated</u> than it was in earlier keyboard instruments. When a key's pressed, a hammer hits the strings. The <u>harder</u> you hit the key, the <u>harder</u> the hammer hits the strings and the <u>louder</u> the note — so there's a big range of <u>dynamics</u>.

2) Pianos have a wide range of <u>notes</u> — up to <u>seven and a half octaves</u>.

3) Pianos have <u>pedals</u> that let you change the sound in different ways.

The <u>soft</u> pedal on the left <u>mutes</u> the strings, making a softer sound.

The <u>sustain</u> pedal on the right <u>lifts</u> all the <u>dampers</u>. This lets the sound <u>ring on</u> until you release the pedal.

<u>Grand pianos</u> have a <u>middle pedal</u> too. This lets the player <u>choose</u> which notes to sustain.

Traditional Organs Use Pumped Air to Make Sound

1) The traditional organ — the <u>massive instrument</u> with hundreds of metal pipes that you see at the back of churches and concert halls — is one of the most <u>complicated</u> instruments ever designed.

2) Sound's made by <u>blowing air</u> through sets of pipes called <u>ranks</u>. The air's pumped in by <u>hand</u>, <u>foot</u> or, on more recent organs, using <u>electric pumps</u>.

3) The pipes are controlled by <u>keyboards</u>, called <u>manuals</u>, and lots of <u>pedals</u> which make a keyboard for the player's feet.

4) <u>Pressing</u> a key or pedal lets air pass through one of the pipes and plays a note. <u>Longer</u> pipes make <u>lower</u> notes. <u>Shorter</u> pipes make <u>higher</u> notes.

5) Organs can play <u>different types of sound</u> by using differently designed pipes. Buttons called <u>stops</u> are used to select the different pipes. One stop might select pipes that make a <u>trumpet</u> sound, another might select a <u>flute</u> sound...

6) Modern <u>electronic organs</u> don't have pipes. Sound is produced by <u>electricity</u> instead. These organs are much <u>smaller</u> and <u>cheaper</u> to build.

No back-pedalling — get keyed in and learn it all...

The sound harpsichords make compared with pianos is <u>jangly</u>. Not a very technical word, but it'll do. You can easily identify an organ sound, though you might not know whether it's a "real" one or an electronic one. Another name for those big organs with all the pipes is the <u>King of Instruments</u>. Isn't that nice.

Percussion

A percussion instrument is anything you have to hit or shake to get a sound out of it. There are two types: the ones that can play tunes are called tuned percussion, ones you just hit are untuned.

Tuned Percussion can Play Different Notes

XYLOPHONES have wooden bars. The sound is 'woody'.

GLOCKENSPIEL — Looks a bit like a xylophone but the bars are made of metal. Sounds tinkly and bell-like.

CELESTA — a bit like a glockenspiel except that you use a keyboard instead of whacking with a hammer.

TUBULAR BELLS — Each of the hollow steel tubes plays a different note. Sounds a bit like church bells.

TIMPANI — also called kettledrums. The handles on the side or the foot pedal can be used to tighten or relax the skin, giving different notes.

VIBRAPHONE — This is like a giant glockenspiel. There are long tubes called resonators below the bars to make the notes louder and richer. Electric fans make the notes pulsate giving a warm and gentle sound.

There are Hundreds of Untuned Percussion Instruments

Untuned percussion includes any instrument that'll make a noise — but can't play a tune. These are the instruments that are used for pure rhythm. It's pretty much impossible to learn every untuned percussion instrument, but try and remember the names of these...

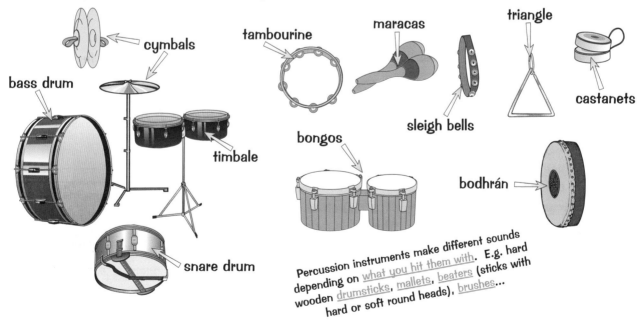

cymbals

bass drum

tambourine

maracas

triangle

castanets

sleigh bells

timbale

bongos

bodhrán

snare drum

Percussion instruments make different sounds depending on what you hit them with. E.g. hard wooden drumsticks, mallets, beaters (sticks with hard or soft round heads), brushes...

Hit me baby one more time...

In a band the point of having a drummer is to add a healthy dollop of rhythm, which makes the song sound like it's going somewhere and keeps everyone in time. In an orchestra the percussion's more there to add special effects — like thundery drum rolls on the timpani or huge clashes of the cymbals.

The Voice

Music being music, there are <u>special names</u> for male and female <u>voices</u> and <u>groups</u> of voices.

*Female **Singers are** Soprano, Alto **or** Mezzo-Soprano*

1) A <u>high</u> female voice is called a <u>soprano</u>. The main female parts in operas are sung by sopranos.

2) A <u>lower</u> female voice is called an <u>alto</u> — short for <u>contralto</u>.

3) <u>Mezzo-sopranos</u> sing in the <u>top</u> part of the <u>alto</u> range and the <u>bottom</u> part of the <u>soprano</u> range.

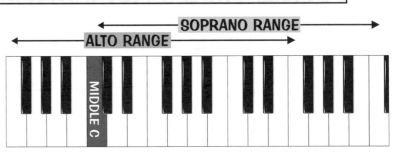

*Male **Voices are** Tenor, Baritone **or** Bass*

1) <u>Low</u> male voices are called <u>basses</u> (it's pronounced "bases").

2) <u>Higher</u> male voices are called <u>tenors</u>.

3) <u>Baritones</u> sing the <u>top</u> part of the <u>bass</u> range and the <u>bottom</u> part of the <u>tenor</u> range.

4) Men who sing in the <u>female vocal range</u> are called <u>counter-tenors</u>.

5) Some tenors, baritones and basses can push their voices <u>higher</u> to sing some of the same notes as a soprano. This is called <u>falsetto</u> singing.

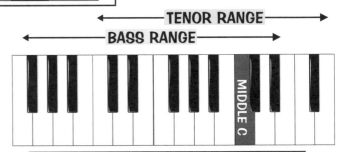

Both male and female singers can sing <u>vibrato</u> — it's when they make their voice <u>wobble</u> slightly, giving a <u>richer</u> sound.

*Children's **Voices are either** Treble **or** Alto*

1) A <u>high child's</u> voice in the <u>same range</u> as a <u>soprano</u> is called a <u>treble</u>.

2) A <u>low child's</u> voice is called an <u>alto</u>. They sing in exactly the <u>same range</u> as an adult alto.

3) <u>Girls'</u> voices <u>don't change</u> much as they get older. <u>Boys'</u> voices <u>drop</u> to a <u>lower range</u> when they hit puberty.

*When **Several Voices** Sing Each Part it's a Choir*

1) A <u>choir</u> is a group of singers. Each part is performed by <u>more than one</u> singer.

2) A <u>mixed voice choir</u> has <u>sopranos</u>, <u>altos</u>, <u>tenors</u> and <u>basses</u>. These are called <u>S.A.T.B.</u> for short.

3) An <u>all-male choir</u> (like the kind you get in a church or cathedral) has <u>trebles</u>, <u>altos</u>, <u>tenors</u> and <u>basses</u>. The treble range is the same as soprano range, so it's basically S.A.T.B.

4) A <u>male voice choir</u> is slightly different — it tends to have two groups of <u>tenors</u>, as well as <u>baritones</u> and <u>basses</u>. No-one sings the higher voice parts.

5) An <u>all-female choir</u> usually has <u>two groups of sopranos</u> and <u>two groups of altos</u>.

These are the names for smaller groups:

2 singers = a duet
3 singers = a trio
4 singers = a quartet
5 singers = a quintet
6 singers = a sextet

No excuses — get on and learn all the voices...

The different voices don't just sound different in <u>pitch</u> — they've got different characters too, e.g. sopranos usually sound very clear and <u>glassy</u>, and basses sound more rough and <u>gravelly</u>.

Wind, Brass and Jazz Bands

In your listening exam, you'll get marks for saying what type of group's playing.
Wind, jazz and brass bands can sound quite similar, so make sure you know the differences.

Wind Bands have Woodwind, Brass and Percussion

1) Wind bands are largish groups, made up of 'wind' instruments —
   woodwind and brass — and percussion instruments.

2) There's no string section. If there was it would be an orchestra...

Brass Bands Have Brass and Percussion

1) A brass band is a group of brass and percussion instruments.

2) A typical brass band would have cornets, flugel horns, tenor and
   baritone horns, tenor and bass trombones, euphoniums, and tubas.

3) The exact percussion instruments depend on the piece being played.

4) Brass bands have been popular in Britain for years.

5) Contests are organised through the year to find out which bands are 'best'. There's a league system
   similar to football. The divisions are called sections. There are five sections and bands are promoted
   and demoted each year depending on how they do at the regional and national contests.

Jazz Bands are Quite Varied

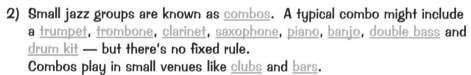

1) Jazz bands have no fixed set of instruments. That's jazz, man...

2) Small jazz groups are known as combos. A typical combo might include
   a trumpet, trombone, clarinet, saxophone, piano, banjo, double bass and
   drum kit — but there's no fixed rule.
   Combos play in small venues like clubs and bars.

3) Larger jazz bands are known as big bands or swing bands.
   Instruments are doubled and tripled up so you get a much bigger sound.
   Big bands were really popular in the 1930s and 1940s.
   They played live at dance halls.

4) Jazz bands have a rhythm section and a front line...

- The rhythm section is the instruments responsible for keeping the beat and adding
  the harmony parts. The rhythm section's usually made up of the drum kit with a
  double or electric bass, electric guitar and piano.

- The instruments that play the melody are the front line. This is usually clarinets,
  saxophones and trumpets, but could also be guitar or violin.

5) A large jazz band with a string section is called a jazz orchestra.

Mmmmm... jazz...

The examiners jurst lurve to set multiple choice questions asking what kind of band's playing, so it's best to
know your stuff. In the real world outside of Music GCSE it's more important to know what a jazz bore is
than a jazz band, so you can avoid him — he'll be all in black, probably a polo neck, and smoking.

Chamber Music

Chamber music is music composed for small groups. It's the kind of thing you hear at fancy weddings...

Chamber Music was Originally 'Home Entertainment'

1) 'Chamber' is an old word for a room in a posh building like a palace or a mansion.

2) Rich people could afford to pay musicians to come and play in their 'chambers'.
Musical families could play the music for themselves. The music written for these
private performances is what's called chamber music.

3) Nowadays, you're more likely to hear chamber music in a concert hall or on a CD
than live at someone's house. Let's face it — most people haven't got the cash to
hire musicians for the evening, and they've got stereos now anyway.

Chamber Music is Played by Small Groups

1) The rooms where musicians came to play weren't enormous, so there
wasn't room for a full orchestra. This meant that chamber music was
written for a small number of musicians — between two and eight.

2) There's a name for each size of group:

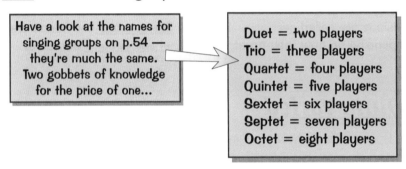

> Have a look at the names for
> singing groups on p.54 —
> they're much the same.
> Two gobbets of knowledge
> for the price of one...

Duet = two players
Trio = three players
Quartet = four players
Quintet = five players
Sextet = six players
Septet = seven players
Octet = eight players

3) With so few people in chamber groups, you don't need a conductor. Instead, one of the
players leads. The others have to watch and listen carefully, to make sure the timing,
dynamics and interpretation are right.

4) Each part in the music is played by just one person.
(That means if you stop or make a mistake everyone knows it was you. Scary.)

Some Chamber Groups are Extra-Popular with Composers

Chamber music is written more often for some instrumental groups than others.
These are some of the most popular types of chamber group:

String trio	— violin, viola, cello
String quartet	— first violin, second violin, viola, cello
Piano trio	— piano, violin, cello (*not* three pianos)
Clarinet quintet	— clarinet, first violin, second violin, viola, cello (*not* five clarinets)
Wind quintet	— usually flute, oboe, clarinet, horn and bassoon

A piano trio has nothing to do with biscuits — shame...

In a way, any small group of musicians playing in a private house is chamber music. But I don't think asking
a bunch of mates round to play thrash metal in the garage counts. Not strictly speaking, anyway.

The Orchestra

If you go to a classical concert, more often than not there'll be an <u>orchestra</u> up there on the stage. Loads and loads of classical music's been written for orchestras so I suppose they have to play it.

A <u>Modern Orchestra</u> has Four <u>Sections</u>

If you go and see a <u>modern symphony orchestra</u> perform, it'll have <u>four sections</u> of instruments — <u>strings</u> (p.50), <u>woodwind</u> (p.49), <u>brass</u> (p.48) and <u>percussion</u> (p.53). The strings, woodwind, brass and percussion always sit in the <u>same places</u>.

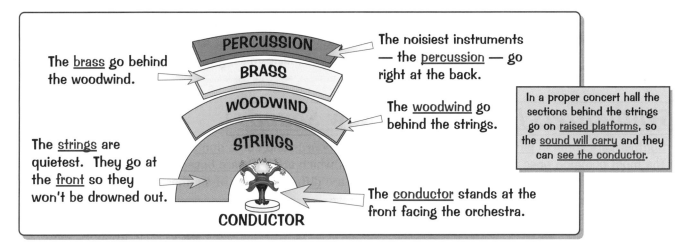

The <u>brass</u> go behind the woodwind.

The noisiest instruments — the <u>percussion</u> — go right at the back.

The <u>woodwind</u> go behind the strings.

The <u>strings</u> are quietest. They go at the <u>front</u> so they won't be drowned out.

The <u>conductor</u> stands at the front facing the orchestra.

In a proper concert hall the sections behind the strings go on <u>raised platforms</u>, so the <u>sound will carry</u> and they can <u>see the conductor</u>.

PERCUSSION

BRASS

WOODWIND

STRINGS

CONDUCTOR

The <u>Conductor</u> has a <u>Complete Overview</u>

1) The conductor has a <u>score</u> — a version of the piece with <u>all the parts</u>. The <u>parts</u> are arranged in a <u>standard order</u> — one on top of the other — so that it's easy to see what any part is doing at any time. <u>Woodwind</u> parts are written at the <u>top</u>, followed by <u>brass</u>, <u>percussion</u> and <u>strings</u> at the <u>bottom</u>.

2) The conductor <u>controls the tempo</u> by beating time with their <u>hands</u>, or a <u>baton</u> — a pointy white stick that's easy to see. There's a different way of beating time for each time signature.

3) The conductor '<u>cues in</u>' musicians — especially helpful for brass and percussion, who sometimes don't play anything for hundreds of bars, then suddenly have to play a really loud, important bit.

4) The conductor <u>interprets</u> the music. A conductor can decide whether to play one bit louder than another, whether to play a section in a moody or a magical way, and whether to make a piece sound very smooth or very edgy. They're a bit like a <u>film director</u> deciding the best way to <u>tell a story</u>.

The great composer and conductor Manuel Du-Pont insisted on the best possible overview of his orchestra.

An <u>Orchestra</u> is Any <u>Large Group with Strings</u>

<u>Symphony orchestras</u> (above) are the biggest type of orchestra. There are <u>other</u> smaller kinds too:

1) <u>String orchestra</u> — an orchestra with <u>stringed instruments</u> only.

2) <u>Chamber orchestra</u> — a <u>mini-orchestra</u>. It has a small string section, a wind and brass section with <u>one or two</u> of each instrument (but <u>no</u> tubas or trombones) and a small percussion section.

3) <u>Jazz orchestra</u> — a largish jazz group with an added string section.

Copper's a good conductor — but Barenboim's better...

Copy out the diagram of the orchestra (without words) then close the book and fill in the different <u>instrument sections</u> in the <u>right places</u>. Then learn all the bumph about the <u>conductor</u> and the <u>different orchestras</u>.

Music Technology

Modern technological and 'virtual' instruments mean that you can muck about with a lot more sounds nowadays than you could in *ye olden times*.

MIDI lets you Connect Electronic Musical Instruments

1) MIDI was invented in 1983. It stands for Musical Instrument Digital Interface. It's a way of connecting different electronic instruments.
2) MIDI equipment is connected by MIDI cables.
3) MIDI data is digital information (i.e. in zeroes and ones). It's sent down the MIDI cables. MIDI instruments turn MIDI information into sound (or vice versa).
4) One important advantage of MIDI is that it's allowed musical equipment to be linked with computers, opening up a whole new world of music-making.

Synthesizers let you Make New Sounds

Synthesizers come in different forms — some have keyboards and some don't.
The most common ones today are virtual synthesizers, which are software based (see below).
The point of them is to let you create sounds. There are different types of synthesizers:

1) Analogue synthesizers were mainly made in the 70s and early 80s. They've often got lots of knobs and sliders — you use these to change the sound.

2) Digital synthesizers started to be popular in the 80s. Most modern synthesizers are digital, though some of them try to mimic analogue synths. Digital synths usually have fewer knobs and sliders than analogue ones.

3) Software synths started to become popular in the late 90s. Software synths are computer programs (often linked to a sequencer — see below). They often have graphical sliders and knobs that you can move with a mouse. Some of them try to be like analogue and early digital synthesizers. They also try to recreate classic electric instruments like the Hammond organ.

Sequencers let you Record, Edit and Replay Music

1) Sequencer is the posh word for equipment that can record, edit (mess about with) and replay music stored as MIDI or audio information. Modern sequencers are usually computer programs.
2) Many lines (tracks) of music can be played back at the same time.
3) Each track can be given its own set of instructions, e.g. instrument or volume levels.
4) One of the big advantages of a sequencer is that it shows your music as actual notation or as representative boxes — this makes it much easier to change and try out new ideas.
5) Nowadays, most sequencers can record audio (real sounds) as well as the MIDI stuff so you can create MIDI music and then record your own voice or instruments along with it. Most music is recorded using sequencers now.
6) Modern sequencing programs often include synthesizers and samplers as well.
7) Drum machines are special sequencers that play back rhythm patterns using built-in drum sounds.

I'm just a drum machine...

Some of this stuff is quite technical — but don't panic. You don't need to have an in-depth understanding of how the different types of technology work — as long as you know what they do and what people use them for. You can even have a go at using them in your compositions if you really want to.

Music Technology

Sampling is a very popular way of putting different sounds into your music.
Samples can be fiddled with and looped to make long repeated sections.

Samplers let you 'Pinch' other people's Sounds

1) A sampler is a piece of equipment that can record, process (change) and play back bits of sound.
2) These sections of sound are called samples.
3) Samplers are often used to take a bit of a piece of music that's already been recorded to use in some new music.
4) You can sample anything from instruments to birdsong — even weird things like a car horn.
5) Today, samplers are most often used to reproduce the sound of real instruments, such as strings or piano. Most pop music is sampled.
6) Pop stars often use samples of other people's music in their own music — anything from other pop songs to bits from Classical pieces. For example:

> • Madonna used a sample of Abba's 'Gimme! Gimme! Gimme! (A Man After Midnight)' in her 2005 hit 'Hung Up'.
> • Take That sampled 'Dies Irae' from Verdi's *Requiem* in 'Never Forget' (1995).
> • Dizzee Rascal used a sample of 'So You Wanna Be a Boxer' (from *Bugsy Malone*) in his song 'Wanna Be' in 2007.

Samples can be Added to Other Pieces

1) You don't have to create a piece made up entirely of samples — you can just add one or two, or use a whole range to create a collage of sound. The collage can then be put over the top of a repeating drum and bass loop.

2) DJs and producers often do this when they make a dance remix of a piece.

> REMIX is a term used for a different version of a piece of music.
> They're often used to turn pop or rock tunes into dance music
> — e.g. by speeding them up and giving them a fast drum beat.

3) Samples can be added to a piece by over-dubbing — adding tracks over the top of other tracks.
You can record a drum track, then overlay the guitar part, then the vocal part, etc.

DJs Choose, Play and Alter Music

1) DJs (disc jockeys) choose which tracks (lines of music) to play, and change bits of them (e.g. by adding samples). Some DJs also rap over the top of the music.
2) DJs play music in clubs and on the radio.
3) At a live performance in a club, the DJ sometimes adds extra sounds using samples, keyboards or a drum machine to build the piece up.
4) DJs use a mixing desk to combine different tracks and add extra sounds to the music, and a set of decks to play their music.
5) The amplification is important — DJs need to make sure the right parts stand out, and that all parts can be heard. The amplification can be changed in live performances.

The dance remix of Beethoven's 5th was a big hit...

Again, there's lots of technical bits on this page. You might choose to use some samples in your own compositions, but even if you don't, you need to know how other people (like DJs) might use them.

Revision Summary

Trrr-rrr-rrr. Trrr-rrr-rrr. [Drum roll] *Pa-pa-pa-pa-pa-pa. Paa-paa-paa-paa-paa-paa.* [Trumpets] Ladies and gentlemen, the final Revision Summary of the final section is about to commence. Take your seats in the auditorium, sit back, and marvel at the wonders of the last page not including the Glossary and Index.

1) What are brass instruments made of?

2) Name three brass instruments.

3) How do you vary the pitch on a brass instrument?

4) Are all woodwind instruments made of wood?

5) Name three woodwind instruments.

6) What are the three different mouthpieces used on woodwind instruments called? How do they work?

7) What are all those little keys, springs and levers for on a woodwind instrument?

8) What's the smallest string instrument?

9) What's the biggest one that you play with a bow?

10) What does *con arco* mean? What does *pizzicato* mean?

11) What is double-stopping?

12) Where would you put a mute on a bowed string instrument and what effect would it have?

13) What makes a harp different from the other string instruments? Give two differences.

14) How many strings are there on:

   a) an acoustic guitar   b) an electric guitar   c) a bass guitar?

15) What do you call those metal bits on the fingerboard of a guitar?

16) Why can't you vary the dynamics on a harpsichord?

17) What's the most popular keyboard instrument now?

18) How is the sound of an organ produced?

19) Name three tuned percussion instruments and six untuned percussion instruments.

20) What's the highest type of singing voice?

21) What's the lowest type of singing voice?

22) What do you call a boy's voice when it's got the same range as a soprano?

23) What does S.A.T.B. stand for?

24) How can you tell the difference between a wind band and a brass band?

25) How can you tell the difference between a wind band and a jazz orchestra?

26) What are the two sections of a jazz orchestra called, and what are their jobs?

27) Why's chamber music called chamber music?

28) How many people are there in: a) a trio   b) a sextet   c) a quartet   d) an octet?

29) How many clarinets are there in a clarinet quintet?

30) Sketch a plan of a standard symphony orchestra. Label the different sections and the conductor.

31) What sections are there in a string orchestra and a chamber orchestra?

32) What does MIDI stand for?

33) How is MIDI information stored?

34) What do sequencers do?

35) What are samples? How can they be used in tracks?

Glossary & Index

There are millions of symbols and tricky words that get bandied about in music. Look up any that fox you here — I've done my darndest to squeeze 'em all in. Follow the page reference to find out more.

Glossary & Index

Glossary & Index

E

edge-tone instruments Woodwind instruments like the flute that are played by blowing air across a hole. **49**

energico Play energetically. **10**

enharmonic equivalent A note with a different name that sounds exactly the same, e.g. A♯ is an enharmonic equivalent of B♭. **5**

episode A contrasting section in **rondo form**. **35**

exposition The first section of **sonata form** where ideas are introduced. **39**

F

falsetto When male singers sing notes in the female vocal range — much higher than their normal range. **54**

fifth The third note of a **triad** — the fifth note of a scale. **22**

first inversion A **triad** with the **third** at the bottom. **25-26**

flat ♭ Symbol that tells you to play the note a **semitone** lower. **5, 15**

forte, f Loud. **11**

fortissimo, ff Very loud. **11**

free metre Music with no particular **metre**. **7**

front line The players who play the tune in a jazz band. Usually trumpets, saxophones and clarinets. **55**

G

giocoso Play in a light-hearted, jokey way. **10**

glissando A slide between notes. **12**

grace note A type of **ornament**. **Appoggiaturas** and **acciaccaturas** are both grace notes. **13**

grandioso Play very grandly. **10**

ground bass A way of playing variations with a strong repeating bass as the **main theme**. **36**

H

hairpin Another name for a **crescendo** or **diminuendo**. **11**

harmonic interval The difference between two notes played at the same time. **19**

harmonic minor scale 8-note **minor scale** using notes from the **minor key** except for the seventh note, which is sharpened by one **semitone**. Used for writing harmonies. **16**

harmonic progression A series of chords. Another name for a **chord progression**. **24**

harmonic rhythm The speed at which the chords change. **24**

harmony Two parts of music harmonise when they fit together nicely. Sometimes the **accompaniment** is called the harmony. **24, 36, 44**

heterophonic In heterophonic music, all the parts have different versions of the same tune. **32**

home key The key a piece starts and finishes in. **31**

homophonic Music where the tune is accompanied by chords. **32**

I

imitation When a phrase is repeated with little variations. Could be one instrument or voice, or two or more, imitating each other. **39, 42, 45**

imperfect cadence **Cadence** moving usually from chord I, II or IV to chord V. **29-30, 37**

instrumental section Part of a **pop song** where the singer rests and the other instruments get to show off. **38**

interrupted cadence **Cadence** moving from chord V to any chord (usually VI) except chord I. **29-30**

interval The gap between two notes, played one after another or at the same time in a **chord**. **19, 22-23**

introduction Opening section of a song or piece. **38**

inversion Rearranging the **root chord** so a different note goes at the bottom. **25-26, 39**

inverted turn A type of **ornament**. **13**

irregular metre Type of **metre** where the beats in a bar are of different lengths. **7**

J

jazz Music with lots of improvisation and **syncopation**. **12, 46**

jazz band Band that plays jazz. Usually has a **front line** and a **rhythm section**. **55**

jazz combo Small jazz group. **55**

jazz orchestra Jazz band with a string section. **55, 57**

K

key A set of notes all from the same **scale**. **15, 24, 36**

key signature **Sharps** or **flats** just after the **clef** that tell you what **key** a piece is in. **5, 15-17, 31**

keyboard instruments Instruments with keys, e.g. the piano, harpsichord and organ. **52**

L

larghetto Play broadly and slowly (though not quite as slowly as *largo*). **10**

largo 40-60 beats per minute. Broad and slow. **10**

leading note The seventh note of a **scale**. **15**

leap A jump between notes that's bigger than a **tone**. **28**

legato Play smoothly. **11**

libretto The words of an opera. **41**

lied A song for one singer and piano. Popular in the **Romantic** period. **42**

lyrics The words of a song. **38**

M

madrigal Song from the Renaissance times for five or six singers. **42**

main theme Musical idea. Usually quite memorable. **35**

major key **Key** using notes from a **major scale**. **35**

major interval **Intervals** between the first note of a **major scale** and the second, third, sixth and seventh notes. **20**

major scale Series of eight notes. **Intervals** between them are: **tone**, tone, **semitone**, tone, tone, tone, semitone. **15, 17, 24**

Glossary & Index

Glossary & Index

perfect interval There are three perfect intervals: between the first note of a scale and the fourth note, the first note and the fifth note and the octave. **20**
pesante Play heavily. **10**
phrase A few bars or notes that are grouped together. A musical sentence. **29, 45**
pianissimo, pp Very quiet. **11**
piano, p Quiet. **11**
piano trio One piano, one violin and one cello. **56**
pitch How high or low a note is. **8**
pivot chord Chord that belongs to two **keys**. It's used to shift a piece of music from one key to another (**modulate**) because it sounds OK in both. **31**
pizzicato 'Plucked'. A way of playing a **string** instrument. **50**
plagal cadence **Cadence** going from chord IV to chord I. Also called an **'Amen' cadence**. **29-30**
polyphonic Musical texture where two or more tunes are being played at the same time. **32, 42**
pop song Popular music. **38**
presto 180-200 beats per minute. Really fast. **10**
primary chords Chords I, IV and V. These are the easiest chords to harmonise with. **24**
pulse The **beat** of a piece — what you tap your foot to. **6**

Q

quadruple metre Music with four beats in a bar. **7**
quartet A piece for four players or four singers. **32, 54, 56**
quaver A note that lasts for half a beat. **8**
quintet A piece for five players or five singers. **54, 56**

R

rallentando, rall. Slowing down gradually. **10**
recapitulation The third section of **sonata form** where the ideas are recapped. **39**
recitative Parts of an **opera** where the characters talk over simple accompaniment from the **orchestra**. **41**
regular metre Type of **metre** where the beats in a bar are all the same length. **7**
relative major The **major key** with the same **key signature** as the **minor key**. **16-17, 35**
relative minor The **minor key** with the same **key signature** as the **major key**. **16-17, 31, 35, 44**
remix When a piece of music is turned into a dance track by speeding it up and adding a drum beat. **59**
repeat Play everything between the signs twice.
If you see this — play the notes in the first bar the first time round and the notes in the second bar the next time round. **35**
retrograde Play the melody backwards. **36**
retrograde inversion Play the melody upside down and backwards. **36**
rhythm section Instruments that keep the rhythm in a jazz band, e.g. double bass, drum kit, bass guitar and piano. **55**

rhythmic chords Chords played in a rhythmic way so you get rhythm and **harmony**. **27**
riff Repeated **phrase** played over and over again. Used in **pop**, rock and **jazz** music. **37, 45**
risoluto Play confidently, decisively. **10**
ritenuto, rit. Slow down immediately. **10**
Romantic Musical style from the mid-19th to early 20th century.
rondo form A way of structuring music so you start with one tune, go on to a new one, go back to the first one, on to another new one, back to the first one, on to a new one... as many times as you like. **35, 40**
root The note a chord is based on, e.g. in a C major chord, the root is C. **22, 24**
root position Playing a chord with the **root** at the bottom. **25-26**
rubato You can be flexible with the speed of the music. **10**

S

S.A.T.B. Short for '**sopranos**, **altos**, **tenors** and **basses**', the four sections in a standard **choir**. **54**
sampler A piece of equipment that lets you record, alter and play back sections of sound. **59**
samples Short sections of recorded sound. **59**
scale A set pattern of notes all from the same **key**. The most common ones in Western music are **major** and **minor scales**. **15-16 44**
scalic Similar to **conjunct**. A smooth **melody** that moves up and down a **scale**. **19**
scherzo Lively third movement of a **symphony** or **sonata**. **40**
second inversion A **triad** with the **fifth** at the bottom. **25-26**
semibreve A note that lasts for four beats. **8**
semiquaver A note that lasts for a quarter of a beat. **8**
semitone The gap in **pitch** between e.g. A and A♯, E♭ and E or B and C. On a piano keyboard, any two notes, black or white, immediately next to each other are a semitone apart. **3, 15, 18**
septet A piece for seven players or seven singers. **56**
sequence Where a **phrase** is repeated at a higher or lower **pitch**. **39, 45**
sequencer A piece of equipment that can record, edit and replay **MIDI** information. **58**
sextet A piece for six players or six singers. **54, 56**
sforzando, sf A strongly **accented** note. **12**
sharp ♯ Symbol that tells you to play the note a **semitone** higher. **5, 15**
simple time **Time signature** with two, three or four as the top number. **7**
single-reed instruments **Woodwind instruments** like the clarinet that are played by blowing between a reed and the mouthpiece. **49**
slur A curved line joining notes of different **pitch**. Means you should go smoothly from one note to the next. **11**
solo A piece for one player. **32**

Glossary & Index

sonata A piece of music in three or four movements for one or two players. The first movement is always in **sonata form**. **40**

sonata form A piece of music with three sections — the **exposition**, the **development** and the **recapitulation**. **39, 40**

soprano voice A voice that sings roughly from middle C to the C two **octaves** above. **4, 54**

sospirando Play in a sighing sort of way. **10**

staccato Play each note slightly short and separated from the notes either side of it. **11**

stave The five lines that the notes go on. **3**

steps Notes that are a **tone** apart. **27**

stepwise When a tune moves in **steps**. **19**

stopping Playing a note on a **string instrument** by using your finger to change the **pitch**. **50**

string instruments Instruments with strings. Fairly obvious really. **50, 57**

string orchestra An orchestra made up of violins, violas, cellos and double basses only. **57**

string quartet Two violins, a viola and a cello. **56**

string trio A violin, a viola and a cello. **56**

structure How a piece is put together. **34**

subdominant Fourth note in a **major** or **minor scale**. **15**

submediant Sixth note in a **major** or **minor scale**. **15**

supertonic Second note in a **major** or **minor scale**. **15**

suspension A type of **melodic decoration** that's made up of three notes. The middle note clashes with the accompanying **chord** then resolves. **28**

swing band A large **jazz band**. **55**

symphony A large piece of music in three or four movements for an **orchestra**. **34, 40**

symphony orchestra The biggest type of **orchestra**. **57**

syncopation When the **accents** are moved away from the main beat. **46**

synthesizer A piece of equipment that lets you create new sounds. **58**

T

tempo Speed. **10, 36**

tenor voice Male voice that sings roughly from the C below middle C to the G above. **4, 54**

tenor clef The name given to the **C clef** when its middle point is on the fourth line up of the **stave**. Used for higher notes in bass parts. **4**

ternary form Type of musical **structure** where the music has three sections. The first and last are pretty much the same, but the middle one's in a different (but related) key. **35, 40, 44**

texture How chords and melody are woven together. **32**

theme and variation form Type of **structure** where a **main theme** is played, followed by **variations** on it. **36**

third The second note of a **triad** — the third note of a scale. **22-23**

third inversion A **triad** with an added seventh, with the seventh at the bottom. **25-26**

tie Curved line that joins two notes of the same **pitch**, so when they're played it sounds like one note. **9**

time signature Numbers at the beginning of a piece that tell you how many beats there are in a bar. **6**

tonality Whether a piece is in a **major** or **minor key**. **36**

tone The gap in **pitch** between, e.g. F and G, or C and D. One tone = two **semitones**. **3, 15, 18**

tongued Separating notes with your tongue when playing a **woodwind** or **brass instrument**. **48-49**

tonic First note in a **major** or **minor scale**. **15**

treble A boy **soprano**. **54**

treble clef The most common **clef**. Used for high melody instruments and high voices. **4, 8**

tremolo Play in a trembly, nervous-sounding way. **50**

triad Three-note **chord** that uses the **root**, the **third** and the **fifth**. **22-25**

trill, *tr* A twiddly **ornament**. **13**

trio A piece for three players or three singers. **32, 54, 56**

trionfale Play in a triumphant, confident-sounding way. **10**

triple metre Music with three beats in a bar. **7**

triplet Three notes played in the space of two. **9**

tritone Uncomfortable-sounding **interval** of three **tones**. **20**

tuned percussion **Percussion** instruments that can play notes of different **pitches**. **53**

turn ∽ ∽ etc. Twiddly **ornaments**. **13**

tutti Everyone plays or sings together. **32**

U

unison Everyone plays or sings the same notes at the same time. **32**

untuned percussion Percussion instruments that can't play a tune, e.g. cymbals or maracas. **53**

up bow V Symbol for **string** players telling them to bow from the tip of the bow.

V

variation Different version of the **main theme**. **36**

verse and chorus structure Structure used in pop songs — verses have the same tune but the lyrics change each time, and choruses have a different tune to the verse but the words don't change each time. **34, 38**

vibrato When singers make their voices wobble, giving a richer sound. **54**

vivace Play fast and lively. **10**

vocal tenor clef Looks exactly like the **treble clef** but has a little 8 underneath it, indicating that notes should be played or sung an **octave** lower than written. **4**

W

walking bass A bass part that moves in **crotchets**, usually either in **steps** or **arpeggios**. **27**

whole tone scale A seven-note scale with a **tone** between each note and the next. **18**

wind band Band with **woodwind**, **brass** and **percussion** sections. **55**

wind quintet A group made up of a flute, a clarinet, an oboe, a horn and a bassoon. **56**

woodwind instruments Instruments that make a sound when you blow them. **49, 57**